BIBLE'S 'BAD' GIRLS...
Stories of some of the lesser known brave and courageous women

Harriet -

May God continue to
give you more peace, love + joy.

Blessings
Danee
11-2-19

BIBLE'S 'BAD' GIRLS...
Stories of some of the lesser known brave and courageous women

◆ ◆ ◆

BY: DANEEN PYSZ

Original dramas about women in the Bible who have done brave and courageous deeds for the glory of God. Using the Bible as my foundation, I bring in historical and thought provoking scenarios both to entertain and enhance discussions.

"… a woman who fears the Lord will be greatly praised." Proverbs 31:30

Library of Congress in Publication Data, Bad Girls of the Bible Act 1, 2012
Library of Congress in Publication Data, Bad Girls of the Bible Act 2, 2014

ISBN-13:9781530386338
ISBN-10:1530386330

Printed by CreateSpace

FORWARD

◆ ◆ ◆

This book is about some of the less familiar *"Bible's 'Bad' Girls"*.

Growing up as a Christian, I was taught many Bible stories; mostly, they were about men in the Bible. This left me with questions as to why weren't there more stories about women? Of course, I knew the stories of the Blessed Mary, Elizabeth, Eve, Ruth, and a few others. However, these were usually presented as minor stories compared to the wonderful stories about men like David, Jacob, Joseph, Peter, John, Paul and others.

So, for many years even decades, I thought God didn't love women as much as men. I grew up in the 1960s when the Women's Liberation Movement was coming on strong. I was influenced by the "women's lib" movement and "woman power!" I didn't know many stories in the Bible that empowered women, and I was taught that the Bible was written by men.

I still believed in God, and that Jesus was my Savior, but I kept wondering why women weren't given more attention. Today, there are many books about women in the Bible. So, you might be asking, "What makes this book different?"

My stories are written in first person and present tense, so you can experience these women speaking directly to you today. My goal is to give you information about these women, peak your interest to learn more about them and simply to entertain you.

I am a wife, mother, and Grandee (grandmother). I was a stay at home mom with part time jobs to help make ends meet. My children and grandchildren are all pretty much grown now, and I thankfully fill the void left with getting closer to God.

Most of my life, I was an entertainer singing, dancing, and acting on stage and in some movies. Nothing noteworthy to boast about. Like Paul, I would much rather boast about the love God has for me and all women and men. Well, my entertainment career didn't go the way I envisioned. God had a different plan.

Looking back a few years, during one of my walks, I started thinking about my life and all the extra time I now had. I began to focus my efforts and concentration on something other than family. I still had a desire to entertain.

I was now too old to be an ingénue. I began talking to my Heavenly Father. I asked him, "What do you want me to do?" A voice in my head, which I believe was the Holy Spirit, answered and said, "Write your own songs and stories about women in the Bible."

Oh, I liked that idea, but my next thought was coming up with a name for this book. Thinking back as a teenager in the late 1960s, I remembered that a popular slang phrase, *"that's so bad!"*, (which really meant *"that's so good!"*) was on most teenagers' lips.

Donna Summers' song, *"Bad Girls"*, also popped into my mind, so I thought of "Bad Girls of the Bible" as a name. I later discovered that title was already taken. I wanted to use something catchy like that, so I made *"bad"* the operative word by borrowing from both the 1960s slang and *Donna Summers' song*. Thus the name, *"Bible's 'Bad' Girls."*

The more I read the Bible, the more stories I uncovered about women who did amazingly brave and courageous deeds all for the glory and honor of God! Like each of us, they had their flaws, but I discovered some very exciting and interesting women. There are many stories about them in the Bible, but sometimes we need to look a little closer and dig a little deeper to find them.

Before I would begin a story about any one of the women, I would always pray for the Holy Spirit to guide me in my research and my writing. I should tell you that I'm an ordinary woman with no ministerial degree. I have a master's degree in management, which I never pursued. I have a passion for research, knowledge, entertainment and the love of the Lord.

I have found, and I am still finding that there are so many wonderful stories to tell about the familiar and less familiar women of the Bible who are *"bad"*. Did you know there are over 200 women mentioned in the Bible with about half of them unnamed? Each has a story to tell. I try to put myself into their individual life situation and ask questions that aren't always answered in the Bible.

The primary source for information was found in the Bible which lead me to be guided by the Holy Spirit as my inspiration. I also researched many authors and their works which I have listed at the end of this book.

Besides a stand-alone read, this book was also designed as a study guide with discussion questions, facts, and ample space to make notes and comments.

I believe God has given me a wonderful gift to share. The Lord has blessed me with the ministry of storytelling about many of these brave and courageous women who have done glorious things for Him. He has a plan for each of us. By reading the stories of different women in the Bible, it is interesting to discover what the Lord's plan was for them and how we can apply their lessons in our lives today.

All those years of singing, dancing, acting and my frustrations of not achieving my goals, ultimately have lead me to exactly what God had planned all along: to entertain and tell you stories.

ACKNOWLEDGMENTS

◆ ◆ ◆

Most importantly, I must give **ALL** the glory to God! Without His guidance and the gifts the Holy Spirit brings, I would never be able to write these stories or memorize them.

Secondly, my husband Dennis, has been my number one fan and supporter. I bounce ideas off of him, he helps proofread my pieces, and when I perform; he is my "roadie". He carries all my equipment, sets up the audio visual equipment, and operates my power point presentations for me. I am so blessed that we can work together for the glory of God.

Thirdly, I must include my children and their spouses; Deena, Jason, Dana, Denyn and Christie who have encouraged and supported me. Also, my grandchildren, Evan, Alex, Nico, Mila and Iyla who entertain me by randomly singing excerpts of my songs, "These Bad Girls Did What Was Right" and "Shaka, Shaka, Shaka the Family Tree".

Finally, my church family, at Gloria Dei; they too have encouraged and supported me through Heart-lifters Bible Study, Adult Bible Study and worship services. Also, the many pastors and brothers and sisters in Christ where I have performed, entertained, and educated with stories of the "Bible's 'Bad' Girls".

My heartfelt thanks to Pastor Sabrina Vasta, Pastor David Mattson, and Pastor Brenda Bos. Their encouragement and interest in my ministry is greatly appreciated.

Thank you also to Art Fettig for his guidance and expertise; and his booklet, "Seeing Your Book In Print."

Cover Photograph:
Christine Pysz

Illustrations:
Cayden Martin, caydenmartin.com

Editors:
Dennis S. Pysz
Dr. Dana R. Pysz
Trudy Daverso

TABLE OF CONTENTS

PROLOGUE 1

◆ ◆ ◆

The following four stories of courageous and brave women are from the Old Testament. Their lives were filled with all the same emotions that we experience in our lives. Each is a testament of their faith in God and how they each matured and grew in their love for the Lord.

Introduction to:
RACHEL

◆ ◆ ◆

Dysfunctional families were nothing new in the Old Testament. Everyone seemed to have their secrets, lies and in most cases, be related to each other by one family member or another. In this story, cousins married each other, and a father was out to get whatever he could to benefit himself first.

When Jacob woke up in the morning after his wedding night, he was shocked to see it was Leah and not her sister Rachel who he thought he had married. *"What have you done to me?" Jacob raged at Laban who was Leah and Rachel's father. "I worked seven years for Rachel! Why have you tricked me?" Genesis 29:25.*

Wow! Talk about some deceitfulness! The story of Rachel has so many layers of emotion. Her love for Jacob was a story gone wild.

Having an older sister, I could relate to some of the emotions that Rachel and Leah probably shared. Most sisters, at one time or another, usually have competition, jealousy, love, hate, happiness and even peace with each other.

My sister, Sherry, never married my fiancée like Leah did to Rachel with Jacob, but we were never really close to each other until after we were both married and had matured. Sherry was eight years older than me, and I was the annoying, spoiled third child. She died when she was 28 years old, but we became really best friends a few years earlier and enjoyed our bond of sisterhood before the Lord called her home.

As I read about Rachel's life, I began to ask myself questions such as: "How could she let her sister just marry Jacob? How could Jacob not know? What was the big deal about the idol she stole from her father?" There are so many emotional levels in this woman's life.

The fact that she was beyond child bearing years when she conceived her first child is another interesting point. Her story, in Genesis 29-35, reads like a modern day soap opera complete with several twists and turns, but the big difference is that God had a plan for everyone in this story.

Praying and asking the Holy Spirit to help me write about her, using Biblical facts, other research, common sense and some imagination, here is my story of Rachel.

RACHEL

The Story of:
RACHEL

Genesis 29-35

◆ ◆ ◆

Let me tell you a story about love, hate, jealousy, rivalry, competition and finally peace.

I was the younger sister. Everyone paid attention to me and said I was prettier than my sister Leah. I always got everything I wanted, but my father favored Leah.

Leah and I never got along, we were so opposite. She liked to stay home and cook and clean and serve. Me, I liked to be carefree and do things outdoors. I loved taking care of our flock of sheep. They didn't argue or talk back and I could lead them wherever I wanted them to go.

Each day I looked forward to bringing them down to the well. I enjoyed talking to the other shepherds as they were much more interesting than the silly, idle chatter from my sister and the other women of the town.

As I approached the well one particularly hot day; I saw a stranger among the shepherds. He did something amazing. He removed the heavy stone covering the well, all by himself. Usually it would take three to four men to lift that heavy stone. Oh, did I mention that he was really handsome, too?

Then he did something really odd. In front of all the other shepherds, this complete stranger tenderly took me in his arms, gently kissed my cheek and then he wept sweetly. I was stunned at his gesture but my heart stirred passionately at his impulsive act.

He said, "I am Jacob and we are cousins. My mother is your Aunt Rebekah". It was love at first sight! He was as wild, impetuous and carefree as I was. We were meant for each other. Our souls just melded together.

We wanted to marry right away. Oh my sister Leah was green with envy. The younger sister was getting married first! Ha, ha, ha! Finally, I would triumph over her!

My father Laban said to Jacob, "The two of you can marry but you must work seven years as payment for her since you do not have a dowry." Seven years seemed like a small price to pay for the happiness that awaited us in our future together. We spent every hour we could together. I no longer cared that Leah had Father's attention. I had my Jacob.

Finally, my wedding day came. I went from ecstatic joy to dreaded despair in just a few seconds. My father forbade me to marry Jacob. He said, "It is our custom that your older sister should marry before you". So, my father, went back on his word and tricked Jacob into marrying my sister.

Now, you might wonder how Jacob was tricked by my father. Here's the thing. I, or should I say Leah, was completely veiled throughout the celebration and even in the wedding bed. My father made sure Jacob had plenty to drink so his senses would be dulled.

As for me--my "loving, caring" father had me under guard for the entire day so I could not make an entrance. I think that's when I decided my father would pay for this deception and trickery.

When Jacob realized what had happened, he was so angry with Laban. Ooh, Jacob had a temper, and he was strong! But my silver tongued, deceiving father convinced him to work seven more years as additional payment for my dowry. Jacob could then take me as his second wife even though he would still be married to my sister.

Jacob agreed to Laban's terms and after his one-week bridal period with Leah, I was given to Jacob.

So I won over my sister again. Jacob loved me more than her, slept with me more than her and made love to me more than her. I didn't like sharing him, especially with Leah, but I knew his love was only for me even though we had to wait seven more years to get married.

His love might have been for me but he also made love to Leah and she gave him four sons in 4 1/2 years. I did not give him any children let alone sons.

How I hated my sister! I felt so incomplete and empty each time she had a son. And to make matters worse, she gave them names to humiliate and laugh at me. She said, "I will call the first one, Rueben, which means, 'see a son'." The next three children were also boys, and with each name she seethed bitterness and contempt. Leah said, "My second son's name is Simeon which means 'one who hears'. My third son is called Levi, for he is attached to us, and my fourth son's name is Judah, which means 'I will praise the Lord'."

I cried to Jacob, "Give me children, or I shall die". Jacob became furious with me. He said, "Am I God? He's the one who is keeping you from having children!"

I was so consumed with envy and anger. I couldn't let my sister win. So I gave my maidservant, Bilhah, to Jacob so that I could have children through her. Our laws stated that after two years without a child, a woman could give her maidservant to bear children. Bilhah produced 2 sons. I finally felt vindicated and I had won over my sister, again!

That didn't last very long. My sister gave her maidservant, Zilpah, to Jacob and with her, he had two more sons. It was obvious that Jacob wasn't sleeping with Leah for her to give him to Zilpah. That didn't bother me, I still won. It was always a competition between us.

I remember one day, all the women were together and Rueben, Leah's first born, brought her some mandrake root and flower. They were beautiful.

A mandrake root, which looks like a human body, was often considered a fertility charm and an aphrodisiac. I asked Leah if I could have some.

In her own selfish, bitter way, she said, "Wasn't it enough you stole my husband? Now you want to steal my son's Mandrake, too?"

She never lets up! I didn't care anymore. In fact, I actually felt sorry for her. I told her, "You can sleep with Jacob tonight if you just give me some Mandrake root." What's one night, when I have him all the other nights?

Well, wouldn't you know it. She gets pregnant again, and again, and again. That "one" night turned into quite a few. God rewarded her with a total of six sons.

When the next seven years of Jacob's labor was completed, he wanted to take his family back to his home in Canaan. My father enjoyed the cheap labor that Jacob provided by tending to Laban's flock. So the two men struck up a business deal where after six more years of labor, Jacob would leave with the speckled, striped and spotted sheep and goats. However, my crafty father attempted to trick Jacob again by having my brothers remove all of these particular flocks out of Jacob's sight to a three days' journey away.

This time, though, Jacob listened closer when God spoke to him, and he in turn, tricked Laban by placing fresh peeled rods of several kinds of trees in front of the animals' watering hole. The flocks would drink and breed there thus producing speckled, striped and spotted sheep and goats. Jacob increased his flock so that it was stronger than Laban's.

By now, we were all much older, more mature and much more tolerant of each other.

I finally stopped being so angry and jealous of Leah by the time her final child, Dinah, was born. All Leah ever wanted was to be loved and respected by Jacob. All I wanted was to give him sons.

Leah and I made peace with each other and became friends--not best friends, but we tolerated and respected each other for who we were.

Then the Lord remembered me and answered my prayers and removed my disgrace. I finally gave birth to a son! I named him Joseph, which meant, "May the Lord add yet another son to my family".

I was so overjoyed. I now knew what Leah felt every time she had a son. We became closer, more like the sisters we were supposed to be.

After 20 years of working to pay for two sisters and livestock, Jacob was ready to take his family back home. A great deal happened in those 20 years. Leah had six sons and one daughter, Zilpah had two sons, Bilhah had two sons, and I had one, and I was pregnant with another child. I knew in my heart that the Lord would bless me with another son.

Jacob felt it was time to leave. Realizing my crafty father would try to deceive us again, Jacob devised a plan. He brought Leah and I out into the field to discuss our escape. Both of us agreed with Jacob and Leah said, "Our father reduced our rights to those of foreign women. There is nothing left for us. He sold us to Jacob and squandered all that wealth on himself."

God blessed Jacob with a great deal of wealth and told him to go home to his father's land. The three of us planned our escape. We quickly packed our children and belongings and headed to Canaan. I still had not forgiven my father, so I took one of his precious household idols. He worshipped it every day. Possession of the idol indicated who was in charge of the household.

I wanted him to feel the sadness and pain he caused Leah and me.

After several days, Laban caught up to us. His wicked, evil tongue tried to convince Jacob that he shouldn't have slipped away. He told Jacob that he would have given all of us a feast and then send us off.

Lies! When that didn't work, he accused Jacob of stealing his idol. Jacob didn't know I had taken it and he invited Laban to search the camp. "If you find it, he said, let the person die."

Hmmmm...that's not good! I had to think quickly. Where to hide it? Mmmmm...I hid it under my saddle and then sat on my saddle!

When Laban came into my tent to search for the idol, I told him, "Father, forgive me, but I cannot get up because I am having my monthly period." Since women were considered unclean during this time, and would not be touched, Laban quickly left my tent. He did not know that I was already pregnant.

However, this pregnancy wasn't so easy, with all the traveling and the fact that I was a bit older.

Jacob and Laban made peace and we continued on our long, arduous journey. I buried that idol and all my resentful feelings knowing that the God of Abraham, Isaac, and Jacob would always be guiding us.

The rest of my story is history. It's really about two sisters, love, hate, rivalry and finally peace. The kind of peace that only comes when you are honest with yourself and the Lord.

BIBLICAL REFERENCE:

Genesis 29-35

FACT:

Rachel was the ancestress of the Northern Kingdom, which was called Ephraim after Joseph's son. (Genesis 48:8-20).

"So Israel has been in rebellion against the house of David to this day." (1Kings 12:19). The northern kingdom is called Israel (or sometimes Ephraim) in Scripture, and the southern kingdom is called Judah.

"...Judah's territory in the south and Joseph's territory in the north." (Joshua 18:5)

She and her sister Leah, were remembered as the two "who together built up the house of Israel" (Ruth 4:11).

She had used the laws of ritual cleanliness to her own advantage. The irony was that it was a lie. She was already pregnant with a son. (Genesis 31:35).

Curious what a Mandrake Root looks like?

Research "picture of mandrake root & flower".

QUESTIONS & REFLECTIONS
Genesis 29-35

1. List some negative wishful thinking.

2. List some positive wishful thinking.

3. What are the pros and cons of positive and negative thought?

4. Why do you think Jacob brought both Leah and Rachel to the field to reveal his plans?

5. Any examples of how we are jealous, envious, deceitful, competitive with others? How is competition bad?

6. Are there any characteristics of Rachel that you identify with? Which ones do you not identify with?

7. Longing or wishing for something—what would you give up or sacrifice for what you wanted? Be careful what you wish for.

8. If you could ask Rachel any question what would it be?

BIBLICAL ACTION STEP:

What action can you do to apply Rachel's courage and bravery to your life today?

PRAYER

Heavenly Father, help us all to learn from the Rachel's and Leah's in our lives. We are all flawed and constantly need your guidance to know the difference between negative and positive competition. Guide us to make the right choices to always reflect the glory of You by being honest with ourselves and trusting you. In Jesus name, we pray. Amen.

NOTES/THOUGHTS

Introduction To:
MIRIAM

◆ ◆ ◆

Miriam, the sister of Moses and Aaron, sang lofty praises to God and led the women in dance and song. She was a prophet and leader among women, and like all of us, Miriam had her flaws and sins. It didn't matter to God. He loved her anyway and gave her wonderful gifts to share with her people.

I didn't realize Miriam lived to be 130 years old! After reading about her life, I was overjoyed to learn that God gave her the gift of prophecy.

"Then Miriam, the prophet, Aaron's sister, took a tambourine and led all the women as they played their tambourines and danced." Exodus 15:20.

Miriam was gifted and talented in so many ways. I let my mind wander as to how Miriam might have felt all those years waiting to be delivered from slavery and being the big sister of two mighty and powerful men, Aaron and Moses.

I love the courage and bravery she shows when she admits her sins of gossip, prejudice and envy. She was not perfect, but God continued to love her in spite of her human flaws.

Miriam was such a strong woman filled with love, compassion and bravery for everyone. There is so much we can learn from her.

Have you ever been hurt by gossip or have participated in that vicious talk? No one wins.

As James 3:2 says, *"Indeed, we all make many mistakes. For if we could control our tongues, we would be perfect and could also control ourselves in every other way."*

Like us, Miriam was not perfect, but her love for God transcended throughout her life.

I used information from the Jewish *Midrash*** story about Moses, along with the Bible, Google, my imagination and inspiration from the Holy Spirit, resulting in my interpretation of Miriam's story.

***Midrash is an early Jewish interpretation of or commentary on a Biblical text. It is a form of rabbinic literature.* **

Miriam

The Story of:
MIRIAM

Exodus 2:1-10, Exodus 15:20-21, Numbers 12:1-15

◆ ◆ ◆

"Sing to the LORD, for He is highly exalted. Both horse and driver, He has hurled into the sea."

That was the first song that was written down and sung to our Heavenly Father. First my brother Moses and the men said it, and then I would lead the women in song and dance as we echoed this praise. Oh, wait, I'm getting ahead of myself. Let me start back when I was a child.

Some people thought my mother, Jochebed and I were the two Hebrew midwives, Shiprah and Puah. Secret names and identities were sometimes used to protect our people from Pharaoh, the King of Egypt, who made us slaves. My mother was a midwife and I began helping her at age five.

When I was around ten, Pharaoh made his "baby killing" decree and commanded, "Throw every newborn Hebrew boy in the Nile River; but the girls, I will allow to live."

My father, Amram, and my mother decided to divorce so they would have no more children. Since father was the leader of the Jewish people, others followed what he did. I told my father, "You are worse than Pharaoh, by preventing any children from being born." Father realized my logic, remarried mother and soon many of the other husbands remarried their wives, too.

A year later, my baby brother, Moshe, was born. Since Pharaoh's order to kill babies was still in effect, we hid three month old Moshe in a basket in the reeds at the side of the Nile River. When Pharaoh's daughter rescued him from the river, she renamed him "Moses" which means, "lifted out of the water".

As the big sister, I was always looking out for my brother Aaron, who was three at the time, and baby Moshe. I bravely watched as Moses was safely rescued by Pharaoh's daughter and cleverly orchestrated my mother to be his nursemaid for the first three years.

I courageously approached Pharaoh's daughter and said, "Oh most gracious and loveliest Princess, may I help you and find a nursemaid for this baby who is your gift from the Nile?"

Even though the Princess didn't know me, she agreed, not realizing that my plan for a nursemaid would be our mother Jochebed. So for the first three years of Moses' life, he was nurtured and taught our Hebrew laws and history by his own mother.

We all had high hopes for Moses. You know how many people have high expectations for their children? Well, my family really believed Moses was destined for something important, especially now that he was living in the royal palace. This gave him the opportunity to learn to read, write and become a great leader. All those things raised our hopes and answered our prayers that he would deliver us and lead us out of Egypt and our oppression. We had been in captivity for almost 400 years.

As my brother Aaron and I became older, we realized that God had given us some very special gifts. Mine was of prophesy. Aaron's was the peacemaking, eloquent speaking and being our Priest. I wondered what gift God had given to Moses, because, at the age of 40, he fled after killing an Egyptian.

One day when Moses was observing the Hebrew slaves, he saw an Egyptian beating one of his Hebrew people. Moses was so enraged that he killed the soldier when he thought no one was looking. The next day when he went to survey his people, he saw two of them fighting. He asked them "why are you beating up your friend"? The man was so angry and said, "who made you our prince and judge? Are you going to kill me like you killed the Egyptian yesterday?"

Moses was afraid that Pharaoh would kill him so he escaped from Egypt.

My hopes for salvation and deliverance seemed to be crushed and destroyed. My baby brother had to leave and escape to save his own life. I was devastated. I did not think I would ever see him again. I didn't even know where he was going. The Egyptian soldiers came around several times demanding to know his whereabouts. Thank Yahweh we did not know. Those were scary times.

Pharaoh ruled with such tyranny. Forty years earlier killing all newborn Hebrew baby boys and now realizing that this Hebrew baby who grew up and was nurtured in his palace, had now killed an Egyptian. Pharaoh was livid and furious. He was so consumed with hate.

No one lamented or wailed when Pharaoh died. We secretly rejoiced and cried to the heavens "deliver us from this slavery! We have suffered for 400 years!" It took another forty years after Moses left and finally God heard our cries and sent Moses back to us.

Words can't describe the excitement, the joy, the exhilaration I felt seeing both my baby brothers joining forces to defeat the new Pharaoh and deliver Israel! I saw the charismatic, infectious attitude that Moses had on everyone.

Moses said, "Miriam, your job is to direct the women and get them prepared for our journey once I give everyone the signal to leave." God also gave me the gift of leadership to organize the women and children.

The new Pharaoh's heart was so hard. It took Moses nearly six months trying to persuade Pharaoh to change his heart. Their 300,000 gods could not compete with our one mighty God!

I'll never forget all those horrible plagues! The water to blood, frogs, gnats, flies, diseased livestock, boils, hail, locusts, darkness and, of course, the worst was the night before we finally escaped. The horrible screams of lamenting and wailing as firstborn Egyptian males were dying. It brought back those horrific memories more than eighty years ago when Moses was saved and other first born Hebrew boys were murdered.

As I helped to guide our people out of Egypt, we abruptly stopped at the Red Sea with the Egyptians and chariots close behind. Moses' trust in God showed us our way out. As he stretched out his staff over the sea, it parted and he yelled to us, "Quickly, the Lord is with us run to the other side. Do not be afraid!"

Safely there, we turned to witness the Red Sea close, killing our enemy. God showed us how mighty and strong He was. We were safe! We were redeemed!

This was where we sang our song of triumph and thanks with tambourines and dancing.

"Sing to the LORD, for He is highly exalted. Both horse and driver, He has hurled into the sea."

Everything was wonderful for the first few months. All the people were celebrating and talking about our escape, the plagues and praising God. But soon the grumbling and complaining started. They weren't happy with the food or with wandering in the wilderness, some even thought their lives were better in Egypt. Even I started to question things.

Moses married a Cushite woman. Now God said not to marry Canaanites or any of the Moabites but nothing about Cushites. The people of Canaan and Moab were pagans and worshipped many idols. God told us if we married any of them, they would turn us away from worshipping Him but He never said anything about Cushites.

Moses' wife didn't look or act like any of us. She was darker skinned, came from southern Africa and she had Moses' undivided attention. Before her, Aaron and I had Moses' attention. We thought God spoke to us too. I didn't feel that way anymore. I wanted that attention back from Moses and the power, influence, equality and the authority I had felt in the past. I was feeling left out from assisting Moses and our people.

So I committed the grave sin of gossip. Oh my, that is such a vile, evil thing to do. And so easy. Just say one little negative thing and the tongue runs wild and can't stop. Pretty soon my discontent spread throughout the camp.

I voiced my opinion to anyone who asked what I thought about his marriage. I would tell them, "I do not understand why Moses would choose someone outside our heritage. She is so different from us."

I was consumed with anger and discontent. Trust me, nothing pleasant came out of my mouth, just mean, negative things.

Everyone was talking about it. Picking up manna, washing clothes, gathering wood, fetching water.... everywhere. My mouth wouldn't stop saying resentful and unkind things about my humble brother Moses. I even persuaded Aaron to agree with me and support me.

I was so worked up. I felt I was right in my arguments. Wrong. The Lord heard what I was saying! I don't know why I didn't think He wouldn't hear. Immediately, the Lord said to Moses, Aaron and me, "Come out to the Tent of Meeting, all three of you". So the three of us came out.

Oh my! Was the Lord going to take my side and restore my authority and power? Finally, an end to my misery! It didn't go at all like I had hoped. He told me He reveals Himself to prophets, which I was, through visions and dreams. To Moses, He speaks face to face. A definite distinction! In fact, the Lord was really angry with Aaron and me. More with me!

I became self-centered and focused on my wants and not God's.

I had never seen the Lord so angry with me! For the first time in my life I was afraid of what He would do to me. He turned my skin white. I was inflicted with leprosy! I was unclean and alienated from my family and friends.

I had to stay outside the camp away from everyone. According to our laws, I had to stay in isolation, tear my clothing and leave my hair uncombed. If anyone came too close, I had to yell, "unclean, unclean!" Now the gossip really spread! The humiliation and embarrassment I felt for those seven days. I was a woman in my 90's. I wanted to die.

Aaron begged Moses to help me and Moses prayed to God to restore my health. He cried out, "Oh please God heal her!" My baby brothers -- protectors and spokesmen for all and still so much love for me even after my transgressions.

Those seven days were the longest in my entire life. It made me really think about what I had done and the gifts God had given me and how I used them.

I remembered thinking back how horrible it was when many worshipped the golden calf as an idol. I used my influence and expertise as a leader while Moses was on Mt. Sinai by persuading many not to worship that vile idol. It was exhilarating how much power I felt which was wrong. I didn't stop them for the glory of God. I did it for my own personal satisfaction.

When Moses returned from Mt. Sinai he gave instructions for building the Tabernacle. It was exciting to see the people working together, using their talents and gifts God had given them and not complaining as much. There were engravers, blacksmiths, masters of gems, incense makers, leather makers; everyone had a job to do.

I was commissioned once again, to organize and lead the women in sewing, embroidering garments and tapestry. All the silver, gold, and fine clothing we were instructed to take from the Egyptian women and other foreigners on our escape was used for this purpose. It was just like when we left Egypt. Moses needed my leadership, my authority. I felt I was equal to him.

Finally, I realized how jealous and envious I was towards Moses' Cushite wife. I thought my lighter, whiter skin was superior to hers so God made me really white Just as leprosy eats away at our skin, jealousy and envy eat away at our soul.

And then I was all alone and led no one.

It was comforting to know that I was still loved and the people waited for me to be healed before we moved on.

Gossip, greed and great prejudice come with consequences.

Even though the Lord forgave me for my sins, I was not allowed to enter the Promised Land. I lived another forty years in the wilderness until my generation died out. We had not learned from the mistakes and sins of our fore fathers who complained and did not trust our Holy Father to protect and guide them.

It's interesting as I look back throughout my life, water has played quite an important role. It has always been the symbol of new beginnings and new life. I helped Moses from the water which gave him new life. I led the victory song after the parting of the Red Sea praising God which brought new life to our people. However, I died in a waterless place. Upon my death, God, in his grace, gave abundant water to the people in the form of a spring which gave them new life.

I realized the gifts God had given me were actually God's gift to His people through me. What gifts has God given you that you can become a gift to other people?

BIBLICAL REFERENCES:

Exodus 2:1-10, Exodus 15:20-21, Numbers 12:1-15

FACT:

Miriam was one of nine women prophets mentioned in the Bible.
(Exodus 15:20-21 Numbers 12:1-15)

> The others are:
> Deborah (Judges 4-5)
> Huldah (2 Kings 22:14-20; 2 Chronicles 34:22-33)
> Isaiah's Wife (Isaiah 8:3-4)
> Anna (Luke 2:36-38)
> Phillips 4 daughters (Acts 21:8-9)

The Assyrians were a great enemy in later years against the Hebrews. Assyrian leader, Ashuruballit, developed the first Assyrian empire during the Exodus in 1365 B. C. (Assyrian International News Agency, Tuesday, October 20, 2015, Timeline of Assyrian History)

The Hebrews clothes and shoes never wore out during their 40-year exodus. (Deuteronomy 8:4)

The Israelites ate manna for forty years. (Exodus 16:35)

The Israelites could have made the trip from Egypt to Canaan in ten days. Because of their grumbling and disobedience, it took 40 years. (Numbers 14:34)

Research "maps of the Israelite's Exodus" if you would like to see the route the Israelites took.

QUESTIONS & REFLECTIONS

Exodus 2:1-10, Exodus 15:20-21, Numbers 12:1-15

1. What can we learn from Miriam?

2. How do you react when you think that God might not be listening because He's quiet, and you didn't get an answer?

3. Do you think Aaron should have had the same punishment as Miriam? Why?

4. Think of times when you have been so joyful that you broke out in song and dance.

5. Do you think we still "pay a price" when we are forgiven or does God forgive and forget? Give reasons.

6. What people today possess Miriam's qualities--good/bad?

7. Have you ever known someone that has been given gifts by God and abused them?

8. What was/were the gift(s) God gave you and how did you use it/them?

9. If you could ask Miriam any question what would it be?

Proverbs 10:19

"Too much talk leads to sin. Be sensible and keep your mouth shut."

Proverbs 15:2

"The tongue of the wise commends knowledge, but the mouth of the fool gushes folly."

BIBLICAL ACTION STEP:

What action can you do to apply Miriam's courage and bravery to your life today?

PRAYER

Heavenly Father, we know you have given all of us gifts and talents. Help us to recognize what we have been blessed with and be willing to share them with others. We know that if we completely trust in You nothing is impossible, for You are always there to guide and protect us. Give us the courage to ask ourselves, "Is this God's plan for me or is it my plan?". We need to do everything for the glory of You. In Jesus' name, we pray. Amen.

NOTES/THOUGHTS

Introduction to

The Story of

A GIFT FROM HEAVEN

◆ ◆ ◆

The Bible mentions six women: Sarah, Rebecca, Rachel, Hannah, Elizabeth and Manoah's wife, all who were old, barren and gave birth when they were past child bearing years.

The Bible has extensive stories about the first five women. Not much is known about the sixth woman, Manoah's wife. You're probably saying, "Whose wife?" Exactly! Manoah is one of the lesser known characters in the Bible but his wife is Samson's mother. She's one of the many unnamed women mentioned in the Bible.

I read in the Bible how the angel of the Lord told Manoah's wife that she would have a son. He also gave her instructions on how to raise him.

Judges 13:1-24 tells the entire story. In verses 2-3, it says, *"A certain man of Zorah, named Manoah, from the clan of the Danites, had a wife who was childless, unable to give birth. The angel of the Lord appeared to her and said, 'You are barren and childless, but you are going to become pregnant and give birth to a son'..."* I encourage you to read the rest of the verses from Judges 13 regarding Manoah's wife.

A birth of any child is a gift from Heaven. After reading about the gift Manoah's wife received from God, I was curious to know what women may have experienced being barren and childless in Biblical times. As I read about each one of these women mentioned above, the same words and phrases kept coming up: "barren," "old," "shame," "their fault" and "God must be punishing them".

I have friends who are childless and some of them have made the conscientious decision not to have children. I wanted to put myself into the life of Manoah's wife and try to understand how she might have felt.

In my research, I discovered that the Talmud, which is the ancient Jewish civil laws and ceremonies, gives her name as Hazelelponi or Zelelponi and that she was from the tribe of Judah. Since this is not a substantiated fact in the Bible, I have chosen to refer to her as she was called in the Bible— "Manoah's Wife".

"A Gift From Heaven" was written using the Bible, research from other authors and guidance from the Holy Spirit. Looking down from Heaven today, this woman from the Old Testament is going to give her first-hand account of what it might have been like to be without a child for most of her life.

Manoah's Wife

The Story of
A GIFT FROM HEAVEN

Judges 13:1-24

◆ ◆ ◆

I am one of the unnamed women in the Bible, my gift from Heaven was my handsome and strong son, Samson. He was my first born. To most people, I was only known as Manoah's wife. I did not have my first name mentioned in the Bible but I suppose it really wasn't as important to know about me at the time as it was to know about my son Samson and the lessons we could learn from him for the Israelites.

Samson was raised as a Nazarite, and he became one of the most famous judges to rule the Hebrew people. An angel came to me when I was barren and announced, "You will have a son. Your responsibility will be to raise him as a man of God." He told me, "I must not drink wine or fermented drinks, eat any unclean thing and must never cut my son's hair; for he shall be raised as a Nazarite and dedicated to God." That is some powerful instructions to follow.

The important story of my son was the focal point of the Hebrew peoples' struggle for survival. The important part of my story, while I waited to have a child, is God never forgot or abandoned me. He entrusted me with the gift of a son.

What I want to tell you about are the emotions and thoughts childless women like me felt during child bearing years.

In both the Old and New Testament being childless was considered a tragedy. It was thought of as an abomination, a punishment, a disgrace believed to be sent by God.

The only area of life that a woman felt she had complete control over, was having a child. She really didn't have any authority or "rights" as women do now.

Today, if a woman cannot have a child, she has options such as adoption, fertility drugs or she can even choose never to have children. She may have career choices, other life goals to fulfill or perhaps she physically cannot have children. The decision to have or not have children is usually a mutual agreement between a wife and her husband.

During my lifetime, my main job and focus in life was to get married, serve my husband and bear him children, especially sons.

Sons carried on their father's name to the next generation. Women were expected to have children immediately.

Most women had no problem bearing children. Some, like myself, were not as fortunate and as years passed us by, we remained childless. Day after day, month after month, year after year, we who were barren waited and hoped and prayed.

Some of these women became angry, bitter and even schemed and plotted for their husband to have a child by a concubine to carry on the family name.

As we waited for motherhood, society would have its own thoughts as to why we could not conceive. Many would say,

"Something must be wrong with them".
"They are being punished by God".
"God has made them barren".

One can only imagine what other hurtful thoughts they may have had and it never occurred to these people that it could have been the husband's fault.

Thoughts of shame and hopelessness played a big role on our minds each time we saw someone else who easily conceived, especially, when they gave birth to a son. Sometimes it was difficult not to have our eyes welled up with tears as we felt a mother's unborn child kicking. The life growing within that mother brought feelings of sadness as we realized there was complete emptiness in our womb.

The women we know from the Bible: Sarah, Rebecca, Rachel, Hanna, Elizabeth and me have such an important story and message to tell. We were the "Bad" girls in every sense of the word. Courageously believing and waiting for God to send us a child.

We felt every emotion from disappointment, sadness, confusion and emptiness to laughter, joy and finally, our long awaited claim to motherhood.

We always believed that God would be merciful and give us a son!

How elated each one of us felt when the birth of our child was revealed to us. An angel appeared to Sarah, Rebecca and me and gave us the good news! Most cannot fathom our depth of pain: physically, emotionally and spiritually that we endured. We desperately wanted to believe the angel God sent to us that our long awaited prayers were now answered.

To some, it was easy, while others like Sarah, first doubted and laughed at the notion. Sarah and Abraham had their one and only child Isaac, when she was 90 years old. Like her, each of us was blessed by God with a newborn son in our barren years.

God used us as role models during our childless years, letting future generations know they are never alone even in their desire for motherhood.

No matter where your life takes you, always remember, you are loved by God and He has a plan for you. He will never abandon you, for you are a gift from Heaven.

FACTS:

There is no specific description of childbirth in the Bible, but knowledge from other sources serves as a guide. Women gave birth in a standing, kneeling or squatting position. Sometimes using birth stones or a birth chair.(www.womeninthebible.net Copyright 2006, Elizabeth Fletcher).

Midwives were significant figures in biblical society. Shiprah and Puah are the two most famous ones mentioned. (Exodus 1:15-20).

Birthing stones (bricks) were used for a pregnant woman to sit upon with an opening in the middle. (Exodus 1:16)

Introduction To
The Song:
A GIFT FROM HEAVEN

◆ ◆ ◆

This Gospel Rock song is a tribute to the six older women from the New and Old Testament who waited, prayed and believed that God would bless them with a son. Sarah, Rebekah, Rachel, Manoah's wife, Hannah and Elizabeth knew first-hand what it meant to be barren for so many years and then to find out God did not forget them.

My song is for these courageous "bad girls" of the Bible who received their "Gift From Heaven" as presented in the previous chapter.

The Song Of:
A GIFT FROM HEAVEN

◆ ◆ ◆

Chorus:
Oh Lordy, Lordy, hear my cry
I'm old and barren 'bout to die
My life seems wasted and not worth much
Please give me a child to raise up, raise up.
I'll protect and shower him with love, sweet love.
Oh Lordy, Lordy, thank you for your Gift From Heaven above.

Beautiful **Sarah** plotted and schemed
Didn't always trust God so it seemed.
She ached for a child to call her own
'til she was old, & barren, and finally gave up
But God did not ignore her cry for a son
He blessed her with Isaac, yes her only one.

Wife to Isaac, beautiful and old
Rebekah waited years for son Jacob we're told.
Daughter-in-law to Sarah, she sought God's counsel
Pleadin' and yearnin', she hoped for years
Humbly implorin', she asks for a son
She's given two, but oh, she favored the one.

Her love for Jacob was a story gone wild
With prayers to the Lord for her to have a child
So much like Sarah and Rebekah we're told
Rachel was beautiful, humble, but no son.
The Lord took pity and heard her cries.
But after Joe and Benjamin, oh, sadly, she dies.

Chorus:
Oh Lordy, Lordy, hear my cry
I'm old and barren 'bout to die
My life seems wasted and not worth much
Please give me a child to raise up, raise up.
I'll protect and shower him with love, sweet love.
Oh Lordy, Lordy, thank you for your Gift From Heaven above.

Oh the Bible says, she worshipped God all her days.
Humbling herself, she sang His praise.
This unnamed woman ached for a child,
As her life grew long she felt betrayed.
An angel spoke to her; oh yeah, that's **Manoah's wife,**
She must raise her son Samson in a Nazarite life.

Hannah prays to God these words so sweet.
"My heart rejoices in the Lord," I will repeat.
Once childless with Elkanah, her loving husband,

She was not forgotten in her evening years.
Son Samuel became judge and anointed two kings,
Mother rejoiced in God's love which is everlasting.

A mother's love she had for her son.
John the Baptist prepared the way for the Promised One.
Her hopeless state led to her miracle,
Because of her strong faith in the Lord.
Elizabeth's joy soared to Heaven above,
Her son was great in God's sight and filled with love.

Chorus:
Oh Lordy, Lordy, hear my cry
I'm old and barren and 'bout to die
My life seems wasted and not worth much
Please give me a child to raise up, raise up.
I'll protect and shower him with love, sweet love.
Oh Lordy, Lordy, thank you for your Gift From Heaven above.
Repeat:

Thank you for your Gift From Heaven above.

If interested and want a free copy of the song, "A Gift From Heaven," please email: daneen.pysz@gmail.com

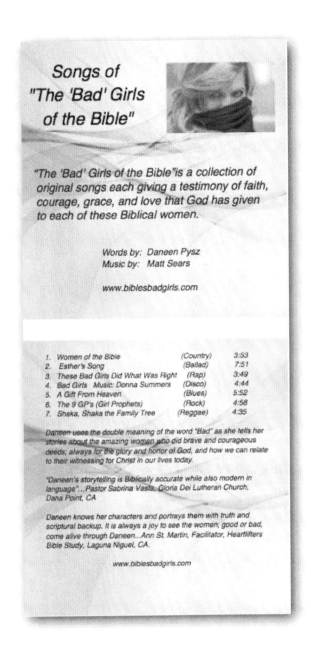

Songs of "The 'Bad' Girls of the Bible"

"The 'Bad' Girls of the Bible" is a collection of original songs each giving a testimony of faith, courage, grace, and love that God has given to each of these Biblical women.

Words by: Daneen Pysz
Music by: Matt Sears

www.biblesbadgirls.com

1.	Women of the Bible	(Country)	3:53
2.	Esther's Song	(Ballad)	7:51
3.	These Bad Girls Did What Was Right	(Rap)	3:49
4.	Bad Girls Music: Donna Summers	(Disco)	4:44
5.	A Gift From Heaven	(Blues)	5:52
6.	The 9 GP's (Girl Prophets)	(Rock)	4:58
7.	Shaka, Shaka the Family Tree	(Reggae)	4:35

Daneen uses the double meaning of the word "Bad" as she tells her stories about the amazing women who did brave and courageous deeds; always for the glory and honor of God, and how we can relate to their witnessing for Christ in our lives today.

"Daneen's storytelling is Biblically accurate while also modern in language"...Pastor Sabrina Vasta, Gloria Dei Lutheran Church, Dana Point, CA.

Daneen knows her characters and portrays them with truth and scriptural backup. It is always a joy to see the women, good or bad, come alive through Daneen...Ann St. Martin, Facilitator, Heartlifters Bible Study, Laguna Niguel, CA.

www.biblesbadgirls.com

To purchase a CD of "Songs of the 'Bad' Girls of the Bible", please email me at daneen.pysz@gmail.com or go to my website: biblesbadgirls.com

BIBLICAL REFERENCES:

Sarah: Genesis 16:1-8 Hagar & Sarah
                    Genesis 17:15-19 Name Change
                    Genesis 18:10-12 Promise of Son
                    Genesis 21:1-3 Birth of Isaac

Rebekah: Genesis 25:19-26 Marriage & Sons Born

Rachel: Genesis: 30:22 Birth of Joseph
                    Genesis 35:16-18; Death of Rachel
                    Genesis 46:19 Sons of Jacob and Rachel and
                    Birth of Benjamin

Manoah's wife: (Samson's mother)
                    Judges 13:1-24

Hannah: 1 Samuel 1:2 Who she is
                    1 Samuel 1:10 & 11 Prays to God
                    1 Samuel 2:1 "My heart rejoices..."

Elizabeth: Luke 1:6-7 Unable to conceive
                    Luke 1:13-18 Foretells of John being born
                    Luke 1:36-37 Barren
                    Luke 1:57-58 Merciful

FACTS:

Sarah was 90 years old when she had Isaac. (Genesis 17:17)

There are two women mentioned in the Bible who gave birth to twins.

    Rebekah (Genesis 25:23)
    Tamar (Genesis 38:27)

Rachel was Jacob's cousin. (Genesis 29:12)

Rachel died giving birth to Benjamin. (Genesis 35:16-18)

The Babylonian Rabbis knew Manoah's wife as "Hazelelponi or Zelelponi". This name supposedly affiliates her with the tribe of Judah. (Wife of Manoah; Samson's Mother: Midrash and Aggadah by Tamar Kadari)

Hannah dedicated her son, Samuel, when he was three years old. (1 Samuel 1:28)

Elizabeth recognized the holiness and blessedness of her relative Mary. (Luke 1:42-45)

Psalm 113:9

"He settles the barren woman in her home as a happy mother of children"

Psalm 127:3

"Children are an offspring, a gift from the Lord"

QUESTIONS & REFELECTION

1. What characteristics do you see in these barren and sometimes older women that are admirable?

2. Which of these characteristics do you identify with? Which ones do you not identify with?

3. What words of comfort can you say to someone who has difficulty in conceiving?

4. How difficult would it be for you to give your child completely to the Lord like Manoah's wife did for Samson or Hannah did for Samuel? Why would it be or not be difficult?

5. Read Hannah's story and about her son in 1 Samuel 1-2

6. The angel told Manoah's wife it was her responsibility to raise Samson as a man of God. That same responsibility holds true to us for our children. How do you cope with a situation where one or your adult children stray from the Lord?

7. If you could ask Manoah's wife any question what would it be?

BIBLICAL ACTION STEP:

What action can you do to apply these older women's courage and bravery to your life today?

PRAYER

Dear Father: You have blessed many of us with a "Gift From Heaven". Thank you for the privilege to care for your little ones. Father, I pray that you will give us the gift of the Holy Spirit through wisdom and understanding for others who do not have children.

Strengthen us with patience, compassion and faith to always know your time for things to happen is always the best. In Jesus' name, we pray. Amen.

NOTES/THOUGHTS

Introduction To:
THE WIDOW OF ZAREPHATH

◆ ◆ ◆

I have never been dirt poor, desperate or completely lonely like the widow of Zarephath. It is difficult for me to comprehend what she must have been going through.

As I read her story in 1 Kings 17, my heart ached for the sadness and loneliness this widow endured. There are people today who are experiencing similar loneliness and desperation. Many of us are compelled to help them, sometimes just relying on our own faith. The word "compelled" is a powerful word meaning "to stimulate, command, oblige or urge."

Without knowing why, this widow trusted Elijah, a complete stranger, and without questioning, she did what he asked of her. It was later that she understood God compelled her with faith, mercy and grace.

Do you remember the joy, happiness and contentment you felt when the Holy Spirit came into your life? The widow in this story felt those same emotions when she trusted Elijah's words, *"...don't be afraid..."* 1 Kings 17:13.

She was afraid and desperate as she only had enough flour and oil to make her last meal for her son and herself. This widow had incredible faith simply believing Elijah when he told her, "Don't be afraid."

I was intrigued as I read her story in 1 Kings 17 of the miracle of the daily portions of oil and flour that God supplied to them. I tried to put myself in her situation. I would have been so excited each morning to go and look in the containers knowing that yesterday they were empty and now they were filled. What an amazing miracle! It is like Christmas coming every day with a present!

Elijah was a Jewish prophet talking and living with a Gentile woman. Not a common everyday occurrence back then but something inside of the widow told her to trust him.

After reading her story, one might ask the question, "How do I know when to trust someone and have faith in them versus when am I being deceived?" I can't answer that for anyone other than myself. My feelings are to pray a lot for God to guide me in the right direction and search for answers in the Bible.

In the widow's case, she didn't know God yet. She felt her life was coming to an end with her last meal and she didn't have anything to lose by trusting Elijah. I don't think she thought she was being deceived. She recognized that Elijah was a man of God. Even though she didn't know his God, she "knew" of his God. That's the miracle of grace and how God can open our hearts and minds to faith.

This is a story of renewed faith and restored life of the soul by having hope and trust in the Lord. The flour and oil is only a minor part of the true miracle in this story.

I pray that we can all be compelled by God to do something for others through Him, so we can experience renewed faith and hope daily in our walk with the Lord.

No one knows exactly how long Elijah stayed with the widow but he stayed until God sent the rains to end the draught.

I have chosen not to give a fictional name to the widow or her son because I believe the story is used as a metaphor for restored hope and faith in the Lord. It is interesting that God chose a single mother and one on the verge of homelessness for this story.

Using the Bible as my primary source, various writings of others, additional research along with the guidance of the Holy Spirit, this is my interpretation of the Widow of Zarephath.

The Widow of Zarephath

The Story Of:
THE WIDOW OF ZAREPHATH

1 Kings 17
Luke 4:25-26

◆ ◆ ◆

Did you ever say or do something completely unexpected or out of character? You simply trusted what someone asked you to do. When this happened to me, I didn't know I was acting on faith. I didn't know what that meant at the time, but with Elijah's scriptures and teaching, I came to understand what having faith in God meant.

Elijah told me, "You and I were compelled by God to find each other." I'll explain that further in a few moments, I'm getting ahead of my story.

I lived in Zarephath in the region of Sidon outside of Israel. Sidon is where the infamous Jezebel lived before marrying King Ahab. Her tyrannical reign and idolatry worship eventually became her death sentence.

That's all I knew growing up--worship Baal and the hundreds of other idol gods. As was the custom, I married at an early age to someone much older than me. He provided for me and protected me. My simple country life consisted of serving my husband, taking care of our home and having children. Soon after I gave birth to our only child, my husband died. It happened just before the great famine.

I was left on my own to raise my infant son. There were no other relatives but I was lucky enough to be able to keep our property and home.

It was difficult being a single mother. Women, especially widows, were not respected in our culture. We were the property of our husbands and if something happened to them, we then became the property of the next male family member. I had no one to help me or give me security.

Because of the draught, my crops weren't growing and I could no longer sell any in the marketplace to help sustain me and my son. It was only a matter of time before we would become homeless.

Rumors of war and hardships of famine were surfacing daily. The little savings I had ran out, and I was soon forced to beg and scrounge in the streets for whatever I could get for my son and me.

My people kept praying to all their gods to send rain but our land just became dryer and dryer and began to wither up.

I was at my wits' end. I believed my son and I would not last another day. I felt like such a failure as a mother. I couldn't protect him, nurture him or provide food for him anymore.

Each day I watched him get thinner and weaker. My son was wasting away and slowly dying before my eyes. I had to do something to stop him from suffering.

I had just enough grain and oil to make us one last meal. I didn't even have any firewood. I gathered scraps of wood at the town gate and that's where I met Elijah.

I was oblivious to my surroundings as I was preoccupied with what I was about to do for my son and me.

Elijah jolted me out of my hopeless thoughts by asking, "Dear woman, would you give me a drink of water and a piece of bread?" How odd, there were so many widows throughout this land, and he came to me.

I didn't know who he was at first. I'd heard the gossip about Israel's prophets and how they dressed and talked. To me, he looked like one of their prophets. Either way, he was a stranger in the land of Gentiles. Men, particularly Hebrew men, did not speak to women in public, especially Gentile women.

I had no hope for the future. I was too defeated and humbled by my lot in life to think of any selfish reply. I simply said to Elijah, "As surely as the Lord your God lives, I don't have any bread—only a handful of flour in a jar and a little olive oil in a jug. I am gathering a few sticks to take home and make a meal for myself and my son, so that we may eat it—and die."

His next words were, "Don't be afraid. Do what you planned, but make bread for me first then use what's left for you and your son. For the Lord says there will always be flour and olive oil left in your container until the Lord sends rain and the crops grow again."

Now you might be thinking, "Wow, that was bold and selfish of Elijah or, I'm going to feed my son first, then I can help the stranger." But I automatically and willingly obliged. I didn't complain or even expect anything in return.

I believed him and trusted what he said! It was that intuitive feeling that I mentioned earlier. I was compelled to simply have faith that what he said would happen.

During Elijah's time with us, he taught us so much about the God of Israel, and that He is the one and only true God.

Elijah said, "God is angry with Ahab for turning God's people to idolatry and not listening to His words anymore. Draught was the threatened punishment of national idolatry. This was how Israel would be punished for their sins.

God told Elijah, "Go to Zarephath and you will find a certain widow. I have commanded her to feed you." His faith brought him into my life.

The moment he spoke to me a new feeling--faith--began to grow in me. Those first words Elijah spoke, "Don't be afraid," those were God's first words to me. My current situation made me afraid but these words put me at ease and calmed me.

The entire time that Elijah stayed with me, I saw a miracle unfold daily in God's provision for us. I diligently prepared our cake with the flour and oil each day. There was just enough for the three of us. No more, no less. It was always precisely measured out.

It was exciting to see this mystery of God's word and work come to life each day. Elijah pointed out the simple miracles God performs regularly that are taken for granted: living, breathing, growing plants, animals, and my precious son. Even the sun, moon and stars where all miracles given by God.

The entire time Elijah stayed with us, he slept in the upper outside room of my home. This insured my privacy and reputation of having a man stay with me. Otherwise, people in town would talk and inquire about Elijah. He was able to privately come and go as he pleased.

Our relationship was one of mutual faith and provision. God, through Elijah, provided the food I prepared it and gave Elijah a secure place to stay.

He taught me about faith and that the Lord is always there to provide for me. I learned about the great faith of Enoch, Noah, Abraham, Isaac and Jacob and how they trusted in God.

For a long time, we only ate bread. It sustained us and it was sweet to the body, just as Elijah's wisdom and daily teachings were sweet to the soul.

Finally, the draught ended and the rains came to replenish the earth as if to wash us clean again. Elijah left us and moved into town. He said, "It is time for me to leave and continue to spread God's word."

My son and I began to work our land and make plans for the future. Life was returning to our normal routine but there was something added in our lives. We now had new hope and faith to guide us, or so I thought.

My son suddenly became sick and died. All my hopes and dreams of a future for my son with a wife and children were cut short. My hopes of him taking care of me when I was old were gone.

I felt as if my life had ended. The despair and emptiness I had during the famine was nothing compared to this worthless, hollow life I was now experiencing. My faith was shattered. I blamed myself for my son's death.

All my past transgressions flooded my mind just as quickly as the rains came to end the draught. I cried out, "How could Elijah come and teach me and then leave me? My sins of my past must be the reason my son died. He was so pure and innocent."

I was beside myself. I blamed Elijah. I sent for him. He found me holding my dead son. I sobbed to Elijah, "Oh man of God, what have you done to me? Have you come here to point out my sins and kill my son?"

Elijah was as surprised and shocked as anyone to see my son like this. He took my dead child from my breast and carried him to the upper room where he had stayed.

I followed him upstairs not wanting to leave my son. I nervously watched and listened to what he said and did.

He laid across my son breathing prayers to God and cried out, "Oh Lord my God. Why have you brought tragedy to this widow? You are the widow's God and do not usually bring evil upon widows; it is affliction added to the afflicted. I pray to you let this child's soul come into him again."

Elijah kept praying to God to restore my son. I knew he had the power to perform miracles. He laid this tragedy on God to fix. Again, Elijah was teaching me. This lesson was to bring our problems to God.

I watched and waited. It seemed to me hours passed as Elijah passionately prayed. He begged God to let my son's life return. God heard Elijah's prayers. He brought my son back to me!

Elijah shouted, "Your son lives!" I couldn't believe my eyes! Here was another miracle that was performed in my humble home! I saw what the power of prayer and the power God has to hear prayers and what can be done with incredible faith.

I joyfully shouted out, "Elijah, now I know that you are a man of God and that the Lord truly speaks through you." He responded to me, "Oh woman! Great was thy faith; one has not found the like, no, not in Israel."

I realized that all the time Elijah was with me, he was teaching me the truths of God's Word and during that time; I accepted them without truly understanding.

It wasn't until my son died that I experienced a spiritual death apart from God. Elijah showed me a new way to live. One day at a time, having faith and giving praise to God.

The restored life of my son was the restored life of my soul and renewed faith and hope in the Lord.

So, I ask you again, "Did you ever say or do something completely unexpected or out of character and simply trusted what someone asked you to do? Perhaps you were being compelled by God to trust your faith."

BIBLICAL REFERENCES:

1 Kings 17
Luke 4:25-26

FACTS:

Elijah (2 Kings 2:11) did not experience death, as he was directly lifted up to Heaven by God.

We do not know Elijah's father or mother or any descendants. (Jewish encyclopedia.com, by: Emil G. Hirsch, Eduard König, Solomon Schechter, Louis Ginzberg, M. Seligsohn, Kaufmann Kohler)

Ravens provided meat for Elijah during the drought prior to meeting the widow. Ravens were known as scavengers who ate rotten flesh. (Fully Revised Fourth Edition, The New Oxford Annotated Bible, NRSV, copyright 2007, Oxford University Press)

Elijah was mentioned in the New Testament: *"Elijah was a human being, even as we are. He prayed earnestly that it would not rain, and it did not rain on the land for three and a half years." James 5:17 New International Version (NIV)*

Elijah was from the city of Tishbe. He traveled to the city of Zarephath, the widow's home. (1 Kings 17:1).

Research a "map of Tishbe to Zarephath" to see how long a walk it would have been for Elijah.

Other bible verses where the Holy Spirit "compelled":

Ezekiel 3:14
Mark 1:12
Matt 4:1
Luke 4:1
Acts 8:39
Luke 4:25 Jesus talks about The Widow of Zarephath

2 Kings 4:1-7 The Prophet Elisha, like Elijah, also helped a widow and her son by using containers of flour and oil.

QUESTIONS & REFLECTION
1 Kings 17
Luke 4:25-26

1. List the characteristics of the Widow of Zarephath and which of these do you identify with?

2. Can you think of someone today that has similar characteristics, i.e., single mom, widow, etc.?

3. Have you ever felt compelled by God to do something? What happened?

4. What miracles in your life have you experienced?

5. How do you tell the difference of trust and deceit?

6. If you could ask The Widow of Zarephath any question what would it be?

BIBLICAL ACTION STEP:

What action can you do to apply the Widow of Zarephath's courage and bravery to your life today?

PRAYER

Holy Father: You are so compassionate and merciful to us. We pray that your Holy Spirit will always compel us to do everything for the glory of You. May Your words always be nourishing to our souls and sweet sounds to resonate throughout our bodies. In Your name, we pray. Amen.

NOTES/THOUGHTS

PROLOGUE 2

◆ ◆ ◆

The next four stories of courageous and brave women are from the New Testament and at first glance, there seems to be even less women acknowledged than in the Old Testament. However, Paul and Luke have included quite a few. Especially in the Book of Acts, we find rich treasures of women with wonderful qualities that we can admire and aspire to emulate.

Introduction To:
DORCAS

◆ ◆ ◆

Her Greek name was Dorcas, but her Aramaic name was Tabitha which means "Gazelle". Talk about a testimony of faith and love! Dorcas was known for her acts of charity, *"She was always doing good and helping the poor."* Acts 9:36.

Dorcas sewed garments for the needy and poor of Joppa. Soon she had many women and even men who helped her sew and serve others for the glory of the Lord. It was amazing how a simple needle and thread could create a tapestry of disciples for Christ.

I can't sew. Oh, my grandchildren think I can! To me, that's all that matters. I can sew simple things, like mend a tear, sew on a button and use the sewing machine to stitch a straight line. When my grandchildren were young, every winter each one of them and I would make pajama bottoms. I would have them choose their material, pin the pattern to the material, cut the pattern and then sew it all together. They were so proud of what they accomplished. Their finished product meant so much more to them than store bought pajamas; even though the store bought ones were sometimes less expensive.

The point I'm trying to make is that it takes time to come together and finish a task. Many hours were spent talking and bonding with my grandchildren. Can you imagine how many hours Dorcas spent with her friends sewing and talking and bonding about Jesus and the New Christian Movement?

Dorcas was a caring, loving and patient soul. It isn't easy teaching someone to sew! It was a wonderful tribute her friends did after she died by showing Peter all the wonderful garments she made for the poor. She was loved and respected by both men and women.

She was sewn into the garment of life, to help spread the glorious news of Jesus' life, death and resurrection to others.

There are only a few chapters in the Book of Acts that mention Dorcas which give a brief insight to her life. Nothing in the Bible is said about her personal life as to whether she had a husband or family. Most people surmise that she was probably a widow. The story is not about her family, it is about her compassion and the love she felt for God and how it reflected in her loving deeds toward others.

I used the Bible and historical research from other authors and a great deal of praying that the Holy Spirit would guide me to write Dorcas' story.

Dorcas

The Story Of:
DORCAS

Acts 9:36-42

◆ ◆ ◆

After Peter's preaching at Pentecost, many people from Joppa returned with the glorious good news about Jesus and His resurrection. I attended Temple regularly and when these disciples preached about Jesus, I too was filled with the Holy Spirit.

I have the honor of being the first Greek female name mentioned in the New Testament. My name in Aramaic is "Tabitha," but my friends in Joppa knew me by my Greek name which was "Dorcas". Since the common language was Greek and not the Jewish Hebrew or Aramaic, oftentimes Jewish people might be given or may change their Jewish name to a Greek version in order to adapt into local society.

Joppa is about 35 miles northwest of Jerusalem on the Mediterranean coast. Joppa had its fair share of widows and orphans. Since it was a seafaring port, there was an abundance of women and children left alone. Many husbands and fathers were fishermen, merchants and naval seamen who lived here in Joppa. Often, some of them drowned or were shipwrecked because of harsh weather conditions leaving their families behind.

My heart ached for all the abandoned and forgotten women and children. Widows and orphans were usually the poorest people and treated the harshest by society. I wanted to help them.

I suppose my epitaph could read; "She was always doing good and helping the poor."

I was considered a philanthropist by many. There were so many widows and children in need of clothes. My love for Christ was so intense. I thought, "If our Heavenly Father loved us so much and gave His Son to die for us, what can I give in return to show my love and gratitude?"

He blessed me with a talent for sewing and making clothes, so I felt guided by the Holy Spirit to help others less fortunate. I was known for my acts of charity, always sewing for the poor and giving money to them from my income selling garments.

I was blessed to have many, many friends. They were my 'family'. My home was open to everyone…whether someone needed shelter, something to eat, an ear to listen to their needs or even to congregate and worship the Lord.

Many of my friends wanted to help me make garments, so I taught quite a few. We would sit and work for hours while witnessing for the Lord.

I remember one time, my friends Rachel, Athena, and her husband Marcus, were helping me finish coats for some needy women.

Marcus said, "Dorcas, I wish you could have been in Jerusalem to see Peter speak on Pentecost."

Athena chimed in, "Oh it was indeed inspiring. We just felt as if the Holy Spirit was received by each person who was listening to Peter speak."

Rachel added, "I felt the same way. Dorcas, you would have been truly touched so deeply by all that happened that day."

"I wish I could have gone," I said, "but I simply wasn't feeling well enough to travel that distance. I'm so glad you are here to tell me everything that happened."

It was amazing how a simple needle and thread could create a tapestry of disciples for Christ.

One day, I became ill and left my earthly body. My friends were so grieved by my death. Someone remembered Peter was preaching in Lydda, only about ten miles away. Two men were sent to bring Peter back. That was about a five-hour round trip. They believed Peter could bring me back to life. Talk about an act of faith and love!

Peter came to Joppa immediately. Now understand, Joppa is out of the Jewish community; Peter was entering into Gentile territory. Jews and Gentiles did not associate with each other. Jewish people believed all Gentiles to be inferior and unclean according to Jewish customs. God was calling Peter to expand his discipleship further by ministering to someone in a Gentile community.

When Peter arrived, several women rushed to him and showed him garments I had made for many people in my town.

Through her tears, Rachel said to Peter, "I wish you could have been here sooner to help Tabitha. She was loved by all and helped so many of the women and orphans."

Athena added, "Look at the beautiful coats and blankets she made for all the less fortunate."

My friends were crying and filled with so much sadness as they mourned my death.

As was the custom, I was laid in the upper room of my home and my body was already prepared with the oils, perfumes and linen cloths. Peter did what he had seen Jesus do on at least three other occasions. He was trained by the Master! He told everyone, "Leave the room". He prayed alone, focusing only on God, then he took my hand and called me by my Aramaic name as he said, "Tabitha, I say to you, get up."

I felt a strange sensation come into my body as if I were waking from an extraordinarily peaceful sleep. The Lord answered Peter's prayers and raised me from the dead!

I opened my eyes and joyously proclaimed, "How wonderfully gracious is our Lord and Savior that He would perform this miracle for my friends." Now the tears of my friends were for pure joy and thanksgiving and praise for Jesus. The news of my resurrection reminded people of Jesus' resurrection, and soon this joy resounded throughout Joppa and neighboring communities.

Peter had returned me back to my friends and community, just as Jesus returned to His friends. The life of the body is one thing, but it is so much better when it is accompanied by life within a community.

I was sewn into the garment of life, death and resurrection in order to be able to spread the glorious news to others of Jesus' life, death and resurrection!

I had the distinction of being called a 'disciple'. A 'disciple' is someone who gives their heart to Jesus to follow Him and learn from Him. I used my talent of sewing to "stitch together" Christ's love for all people. Life goes on after we leave this earth, but our legacy and memory remains, like a remnant of cloth, with others whose lives we have touched.

I know that many in my community of Joppa shared the same love and passion for Christ that I did. I taught many women and men to "stitch for Christ" and continue their faith for Jesus. The miracle of my resurrection caused many to believe in the Lord.

What legacy and memory will you leave for others?

BIBLICAL REFERENCES:

Acts 9:36-42

FACT:

Many Jews living in the Diaspora (outside Judaea) had two names, one Jewish and one Greek or Latin. (www.womeninthebible.net Copyright 2006 Elizabeth Fletcher). This helped with the assimilation of Jews in the Greek communities and also Greek was the dominate language of the world.

Abram was changed to Abraham (Genesis 17:5)

His wife, Sarai, her name was changed to Sarah (Genesis 17:15)

Joseph's name was changed to Zaphenath-paneah (Genesis 41:45)

Jedidiah was the original name for Solomon (2 Samuel 12:24-25)

God gave Jacob the name Israel
(Genesis 32:28)

Esther was also known as Hadassah
(Esther 2:7)

Dorcas in Greek means: "a female roe deer".

Peter had three names: Cephas, Simon and Peter.
(John 1:42 and Matthew 4:18)

Peter was also called The Rock (Matthew 16:18)

Paul had two names: Saul and Paul.
(Acts 13:9)

To see a larger list of name changes, go to:
godwords.org

The original Greek text describes this widowed-woman as 'mathetria,' a female disciple - the only time the New Testament uses this word. (Acts 9:36, Thayer and Smith. "Greek Lexicon entry for Mathetria". "The New Testament Greek Lexicon")

Dorcas is the only woman mentioned in the Bible to be raised from the dead. (Acts 9:40)

The Dorcas Society is named after Dorcas. They are an organization that provides clothing to the poor and needy. The earliest one established was in the 1800's. There are many throughout the world. (Wikipedia)

Look up the website: dorcas-cary.org/ to learn more about the Dorcas Society.

QUESTIONS & REFLECTIONS
Acts 9:36-42

1. What are the characteristics of Dorcas? Which ones do you identify with?

2. What talents do you have to share with others for Jesus?

3. Why doesn't the Bible tell us more details about Dorcas' life?

4. Why do you think Dorcas wasn't quoted in the Bible?

5. Who and what are the 10 occasions of people mentioned in the Bible who are raised from the dead?

    a. 1 Kings 17:22
    b. 2 Kings 4:34-35
    c. 2 Kings 13:20-21
    d. Luke 7:14-15
    e. Luke 8:52-56
    f. John 11:43-44
    g. Matthew 28:6; Acts 2:24
    h. Matthew 27:52
    i. Acts 9:40
    j. Acts 20:7-12

6. What do you want your epitaph to say?

7. If you could ask Dorcas any question what would it be?

BIBLICAL ACTION STEP:

What action can you do to apply Dorcas' courage and bravery in your life today?

PRAYER

Father, you are the glorious creator of all things and we praise and glorify you. Help us to look for the good in others and be stitched together with your love and blessings so that we may be instruments of peace to magnify your Holiness. In Jesus' name, we pray. Amen.

NOTES/THOUGHTS

Introduction To:
LYDIA

◆ ◆ ◆

Lydia was the first woman convert to Christianity and charter member of the Church of Philippi. *"…if you believe me to be faithful to the Lord, come to my house and stay".* Acts 15:16.

Hospitality is a wonderful gift to give. Paul must have found Lydia, his new friend and convert, to be a very loving and faithful woman; for he stayed with her quite a long time.

Good thing Benjamin Franklin wasn't around at the time, for he is quoted as saying, "Guests, like fish, begin to smell after three days."

I don't agree with Ben Franklin as much as I support Lydia's generosity. All through my married life, my husband and I have had guests who stayed well over three days on many occasions and they didn't smell like fish. Occasionally, we encountered some odd mannerisms, but that's part of the enjoyment of hospitality—getting to know your guests.

The best times were when our children were growing up and they would ask for a friend to sleep over or have dinner with us. It made us feel good to know that our children loved our family environment and felt so comfortable with us because they wanted to share that warmth and hospitality with others.

Jesus tells us to *"love one another."* John 13:34. What better way is there to do that than to be kind, thoughtful and hospitable. It's a wonderful gift and one that God has given us all. Lydia's life was the perfect model to pattern examples of hospitality.

Lydia's story is so inspiring. As I read about her, I imagined what life must have been like in the First Century and to actually meet the Apostle Paul. Try to equate it with meeting someone famous today that would come and stay with you.

The Bible, and being guided by the Holy Spirit, were my two main sources of inspiration for this story. The Internet was great for basic facts about the color of purple and how it's made.

Lydia's home became the gathering place for teaching, fellowship, communion and prayer. Purple became synonymous with passion, wealth and royalty. Christ's words and His life became the color purple in her life, with brilliant shades of crimson which reflected His Passion, His Richness, His Royalty and the wealth of our inheritance of Heaven. Hospitality is a powerful gift!

Lydia

The Story Of:
LYDIA

Acts 16:13-15

◆ ◆ ◆

"If you believe me to be faithful to the Lord, come to my house and stay."

These were the words I spoke to Paul just after my entire household and I were baptized in the Holy Spirit by him. I will explain this a little later. First let me tell you a little bit about myself.

I was originally from a small textile town called Thyatira, which was a province of Lydia in Asia Minor. I was named after this province. Our town was famous for purple dye. It was made from shellfish. The fluid from them was first placed on wool, which turned it blue. Then it was exposed to the sunlight, which turned it green and finally purple. When it was washed in water, it became a brilliant crimson. It was indeed very difficult and time consuming to make. One would need a great deal of wealth to purchase a purple garment or robe.

Purple became synonymous with passion, royalty and wealth. Only the very wealthy and kings could afford this garment of color. Even though my town produced the dye, I needed to move to the city of Philippi which was on the coastline of the Aegean Sea to become successful in my textile business. Philippi became one of the great import/export merchants of this unique cloth to Europe. As a business owner, I knew many people in Philippi and I became known as "Lydia from Thyatira" who produced the color purple.

As one of the few single, female merchants in town, I was respected by women and men. There were many Jewish and Greek people living in Philippi and as a Greek, I became well acquainted with Jewish, God fearing women. I was part of their worship meetings even before I converted to Judaism.

We would gather regularly near the riverbank worshipping God. This was the only type of meeting place we were allowed by the Romans. There were more Jewish women than Jewish men in Philippi, so we had no synagogues. Jewish law stated the requirement of ten male heads of households to be in regular attendance to worship in a synagogue.

Paul, and his three disciples, Silas, Luke and Timothy, found our small group of women worshipping one Sabbath day near the riverbank. He introduced himself and began to tell us about the Messiah.

As soon as Paul began to speak, the Lord opened my heart to heed the things he said. He spoke of the history of the Jewish people in the Old Testament culminating in the coming of Christ, which means "Messiah". He also told us of the life, crucifixion and the resurrection of Jesus of Nazareth, who was the Messiah prophesied in the Old Testament.

Paul passionately proclaimed, "Jesus is the long awaited Messiah. He is the one the prophets spoke about. He has come for both Jews and Gentiles.

He has sent His Advocate, the Holy Spirit to be with you. Your sins are forgiven. Come, be baptized in the Holy Spirit."

I was filled with the joy and excitement of the Holy Spirit. I wanted to learn more, to know more. I wanted to be entirely bathed in the love, grace and forgiveness of Jesus. My faith burned like hot embers on an unquenchable fire. I was ready. I wanted to be baptized as soon as he finished preaching.

And I was! I was so happy on the day of my baptism that my heart became filled with the Holy Spirit.

I was completely immersed in water. The moment Paul finished baptizing me, I felt a great weight lifted from me and the feelings of peace and joy flooded my being. I felt as though I was washed clean on the inside and I felt as though my new self, sparkled and shined with the grace of God. Many others were also baptized that day. I didn't want Paul to leave. I wanted to learn more so I invited him to stay at my home.

Filled with compassion, I said to him, "If you believe me to be faithful to the Lord, come to my house and stay."

My lucrative textile business in Philippi afforded me many benefits other single women could not achieve. My household of servants, both men and women, encompassed a large enough upper room with a separate entrance. This allowed me the freedom to invite Paul and his travelers to stay in my house for quite a few months without scandal.

What wonderful gatherings we had as Paul continued to preach the Gospel to us. Each evening he would tell us stories about his faith through Jesus. One of my favorite stories was his conversion of faith and baptism.

Paul confessed, "At first I persecuted all of Jesus' followers. I hated them because Jesus was teaching different views such as acceptance and love for women and poor people and even for Gentiles. I watched as His disciple Stephen was stoned to death. I held the coats of my fellow teachers as they threw rocks that killed him. This persecution and murderous threats to the new Christians went on for several months until one day on the road to Damascus Jesus spoke to me!"

Paul continued, "A light from heaven flashed around me and I fell to the ground and heard a voice saying, "Saul, Saul, why do you persecute me?"

"Who are you, Lord?" I asked.

"I am Jesus," He replied. "Now get up and go into the city, and you will be told what you must do."

"For three days I could not see. I was blinded! I didn't eat or drink anything in those three days. My men led me to the city and a man named Ananias came to me. He placed his hands on me and restored my sight."

Ananias told me, "Brother Saul, the Lord Jesus, who appeared to you on the road as you were coming here has sent me so that you may see again and be filled with the Holy Spirit."

"Immediately, something like scales fell from my eyes and I could see again! I was then baptized by the disciples in Damascus. My name was changed from Saul to Paul".

The change in Paul's name from Saul can be confusing. Saul was his Jewish birth name and dealt with the past. When he was baptized in the Holy Spirit, the feeling of rebirth and newness filled him, and by the grace of God, Saul's name was changed to the Gentile name of Paul. Jesus wanted him to bring the Good News to the Gentiles. Again, this was another example of relating better to the people to whom he would be preaching.

When Paul would speak we would become energized through his words and we ached to learn more about Jesus. I witnessed how our small group of women continued to grow with converts of Romans, Gentiles and Jews.

Christ's words and life became the color purple in our lives. The "shellfish" is symbolic of God who made us. We are the "wool," and the "fluid" as Jesus' blood turns us different colors until we are washed in baptism of the Holy Spirit. Our lives became brilliant shades of crimson which reflect His Passion, His Richness, His Royalty and the wealth of our inheritance of Heaven.

Paul believed me to be faithful to the Lord. Jesus said, "You shall love the Lord your God with all your heart, with all your soul, and with all your mind," and I did.

When Paul continued on his missions, he kept us in his prayers. His letters to our church in Philippi were always encouraging and enlightening. All churches everywhere at times have conflicts and struggles within.

Paul said, "Rejoice in the Lord and let our gentleness be known to everyone. You should not worry about anything, but everything by prayer and supplication with thanksgiving let your requests be made known to God."

I was a single woman with only a few privileges in the first century but I had the honor of being Paul's first woman convert to Christianity and a charter member of the Church of Philippi.

The only way I knew how to show the love and joy I felt was to give what I could and open my home to others who needed to know Jesus. My heart was opened to Christ on the day of my baptism which overflowed my spirit with all the brilliant shades of purple.

Hospitality is a powerful gift!

BIBLICAL REFERENCES:

Acts 16:13-15

FACT:

The hospitality of Lydia can also be compared to the Shulamite Woman (2 Kings 4:8-37).

Jewish law stated ten male heads of households who could be in regular attendance were required for a synagogue.

Lydia is the first person recorded to have been saved in Europe.

Lydia's conversion marks the beginning of a new era in the Bible of including Gentiles in salvation and God's Plan for each of us as Paul's ministry was for Gentiles, too.

Archaeologists have found among the ruins of Thyatira inscriptions relating to a dyers' guild in the city. This is an organized group of merchant dyers.

Paul had three missionary journeys. The first was to Antioch in Syria, the second was Greece (which included Philippi) and the third was Asia Minor.

QUESTIONS & REFLECTION

Acts 16:13-15

1. Which of these characteristics of Lydia do you identify with? Why?

    a. she was a woman of prayer
    b. she listened and was eager to learn
    c. she was a worshipper
    d. she opened her heart
    e. she was obedient to baptism
    f. she confessed that she was a believer
    g. she wanted to serve
    h. she opened her home
    i. she was hospitable

2. What does it mean to "heed" the word of God?

3. What would be the first thing you would tell someone who asked about Jesus?

4. What does it mean to listen, believe, obey and serve God?

5. If you could ask Lydia any question what would it be?

BIBLICAL ACTION STEP:

What action can you do to apply Lydia's courage and bravery to your life today?

PRAYER

Dear Jesus: I want to be more like you. Washed in the baptism of your love for me and filled with the joy and peace of the Holy Spirit. Help me to show hospitality to others through teaching, fellowship, communion, and prayer. Bless me with burning desire in my heart to always show love to others. In your name, I pray. Amen.

NOTES/THOUGHTS

Introduction To:
PRISCILLA

◆ ◆ ◆

Our Bible study group, Heart Lifters, attempted to use one hour to discuss Dorcas (also known as Tabitha), Lydia and Priscilla, but one hour was not enough time to tell their stories. The story of these three women, required more of an in depth view of their contribution to Christianity that was embraced in the first century AD. As you can see by the two previous stories, which were about Dorcas and Lydia, and this story about Priscilla, each woman had an important message to share. These women had qualities of courage, bravery and their lives were dedicated to the Lord.

Priscilla's life is unique due to the fact that she is the only married woman that the Apostle Paul mentions. He recognized her love for Christ, for she was very dedicated in her worship, learning and teaching about Jesus.

She and her husband, Aquila, led worship services and were in the same business, which was tent making, working together each and every day.

There is no mention of children, but I believe their lives were enriched by the love they had for each other and for Christ. This brings me to an important observation about Priscilla and Aquila. They made a good team.

It is encouraging to read in the New Testament about a husband and wife who so loved the Lord. What a wonderful role model they are for many of us today. They worked together, prayed together and trusted God that the Holy Spirit would always guide them on their journeys through life.

Priscilla and Aquila are never quoted in the Bible but Paul must have had a great deal of respect and admiration for them. Their story can be found in the Book of Acts and briefly mentioned in Romans, 1 Corinthians and 2 Timothy.

For example, in Romans 16:4, Paul writes about Priscilla and Aquila: *"In fact, they once risked their lives for me."* What a wonderful testimony he gave about these two people. He must have been bragging about them everywhere he went. They opened their home to Paul and the new believers.

Studying primarily the chapters in Acts, along with the inspiration of the Holy Spirit, I was definitely guided in writing this story about Priscilla. I threw in a few historical facts, which I researched, so that you could get more of a perspective of the time when she lived. This is what I think she might have been feeling and say

Priscilla

The Story Of:
PRISCILLA

Acts 18:1-3, Acts 18:18-26, Romans 16:3,
1 Corinthians 16:19, 2 Timothy 4:19

◆ ◆ ◆

First Century AD was both an exciting and dangerous time to live. The 'Jesus Movement' or the "Christian Revolution," or what we called "The Way" was beginning to take on some solid roots. A few years earlier, in Jerusalem, our Pentecostal celebration took on an entirely new meaning. On that day, the Holy Spirit appeared to the Apostles and blessed them with many gifts. One was the ability to announce Jesus' Resurrection to all nations in native languages. This good news spread throughout the neighboring Jewish communities and resonated into the Gentile communities.

My husband, Aquila and I, were living in Rome at the time. I'm Prisca, but my friends call me Priscilla. In 49 AD, Emperor Claudius deported all the Jews from Rome. It was just another exodus cleansing that our Jewish heritage knew only too well.

Aquila and I were tentmakers, by trade. We had a very lucrative and profitable business in Rome and a lovely villa in our Jewish community. Our work and our lives were encompassed by our love for God, which gave our marriage a strong foundation.

I told Aquila, "As much as I love it here and we have a comfortable life, I believe God is calling us to a new direction to seek out other believers." Aquila agreed with me and said, "My dearest love, through prayer we will seek the Lord's guidance as we have done in everything in our lives."

Many of us decided to settle in Corinth which was about a 600-mile journey. It was located between Rome and Asia Minor. A great commercial city with a double harbor, however, the city had a bad reputation of loose morality, and promiscuous activity.

We felt confident that God would send the Holy Spirit to guide us in our travels to our new home and help us to establish our tent business.

That is what made our marriage so strong, we took all our questions, fears, conflicts, joys and happy moments together in prayer to the Lord to ask for guidance.

Tent making was honest, hard work, and very satisfying. Aquila and I worked side by side designing and creating tents to sell. They were made from goat hair, which is heavy and thick, and it is woven in strips on large looms. I would weave the fabric for the tents then stitch them together. Cutting the fabric precisely was as important as hearing and teaching the Gospel correctly.

We spent many hours together stitching, talking and asking each other questions about God and the Messiah and wanting to hear from some of the Apostles. We felt isolated and alone from hearing more of the Good News.

Aquila would say, "Wouldn't it be exciting to hear what the Apostles are preaching now?"

I would reassure him by saying, "We will. God led us to Corinth for a reason. He has plans for us and work to do. We just don't know what that is, yet."

Since many of our people and even Gentiles lived nomadic lives, our business was always in demand. That's how we met Paul. We had heard about his great ministry so when we learned about his arrival, we went to hear him preach. The three of us became fast friends with our commonality of tent making and our Christ centered lives.

Paul stayed with us for two and a half years. It was wonderful having him and his fellow disciples, Silas, Timothy and Luke working so closely with us and others to establish the first Christian Church in Corinth.

When Paul was ready to embark on another mission, he said, "Aquila, I would like to invite you and Priscilla to go with me to spread the Gospel."

Aquila said, "We are honored and humbled that you think so highly of us that we could be disciples and missionaries in other parts of the world! Priscilla, do you agree that we should embark on this mission?"

I told Aquila, "Yes, most definitely." Turning to Paul I said, "Bless you, Paul. We have been praying to God for guidance and direction and He has brought you into our lives."

The Holy Spirit guided us on a short trip to Syria and then finally to Ephesus. It was centrally located along the coast of Asia Minor, just about five miles inland from the Aegean coast. Ephesus attracted many influential Christian and philosophical leaders.

We certainly weren't welcomed with open arms! Many embraced Paul's teachings but there were still some in the Jewish and Greek communities who created as much trouble as they could. Sosthenes and Demetrius were just two of the ring leaders. These two men were the leading proprietors for manufacturing and selling statues of the Greek goddess, Artemis.

Demetrius complained to the local council, "Paul is taking away the prestige of Artemis. She is known the world over but Paul is preaching about salvation through this person named Jesus."

Demetrius was more concerned about his business than the idol but all his yelling and commotion did not stop Paul.

There was one bright shining star. His name was Apollos. He was an eloquent speaker, but knew only of John the Baptist's ministry. He had travelled all the way from Alexandria, Egypt. He was highly educated in the Jewish scripture and some of the early Christian teachings, but he was missing the greatest part of the story: Jesus' life, death and resurrection.

Just as Paul, Aquila and I cut the cloth precisely for the tents we made, we spoke the Gospel with precision and exactness and strength.

I told Aquila and Paul, "Apollos needs to be educated about Jesus' life and Resurrection. I believe the Holy Spirit brought Apollos into our lives so that we can guide him further in his ministry".

Paul agreed and said, "Apollos is indeed a powerful speaker. I know that you are both faithful servants of God and He will guide you as you teach him."

Aquila and I were so blessed that our home was the church or gathering place in Ephesus. I loved teaching anyone who would listen about Christ. Women were not permitted to teach in public, but in my home, I was a strong and reliable voice. Paul encouraged me to use my voice for Jesus. I took it upon myself to teach Apollos about Jesus.

Sitting together in our home in the evenings, I earnestly told Apollos, "The Holy Spirit has given you the wonderful gift of preaching. Jesus said that He would send the Holy Spirit to be an Advocate for us."

Apollos questioned, "Who is the Holy Spirit?"

I explained to him the Trinity and said, "The Holy Spirit gives us gifts and the fruit of the Spirit. Each person has a gift of either wisdom, knowledge, faith, healing, power to do miracles, prophesy, speaking in unknown languages, interpretation of languages or tongues. He gives discernment to know whether a message is from God or some other spirit."

Apollos listened intently and soaked up every piece of information. He was a quick study. He inquired, "What is the fruit of the Spirit?"

I furthered explained, "The fruit of the Spirit is peace, love, joy, patience, kindness, goodness, faithfulness, gentleness and self-control."

The Holy Spirit was burning within our hearts. God used me as an instrument, like a strong, sturdy tent for which Apollos could rely on for strong truth and sturdy knowledge about our Lord and Savior.

"Did you know Jesus and a tent have many of the same characteristics?" I continued, "Both give warmth, comfort and shelter. They are both a dwelling and you can take either of them wherever you go."

The Holy Spirit inspired Apollos to make a mission trip to Achaia. We encouraged him to go and we sent a letter of recommendation asking the believers in Achaia to welcome him. We felt confident that Apollos would be a great benefit to the people there.

Shortly after Apollos had left and Paul was in Greece, we felt the Holy Spirit guiding us back to Rome.

Aquila said to me, "Emperor Claudius is now dead, so it seems safe to return to our former home. You and I keep hearing about the new Christians in Rome so let's go back. We have both been longing to be a part of their ministry."

I was excited for our return and agreed, "Yes, I think the time is right. Let's pray and ask God for guidance."

Paul was delighted when we returned to Rome and wrote letters supporting us in our mission. Even before we were settled, our home became the meeting place for worship with our new Gentile brothers and sisters in Christ.

Our beloved friend, Paul, was so grateful for the many times we helped him. We visited him and tended to any needs he had through his many encounters with Roman authority which ultimately landed him in prison. We loved him so much and would risk our lives for him; just as he and Barnabas had done for the sake of Jesus.

The last time we spoke with Paul was during his final time in prison in Rome. He confided in us, "I believe God has brought me to exactly where he wants me. I have run the good race and I believe the Lord sees me as His good and faithful servant."

Nero, the current Emperor of Rome, was crazy and intent on persecuting all the Christians in Rome. We escaped back to Ephesus. Even in his final letter, Paul lovingly and selflessly remembered his friends.

Aquila and I had a wonderful marriage and life together. We encouraged and supported each other in our business and our passion for Jesus. One thing is for certain, our marriage was bound in love. We will never forget Paul. Just as Paul stretched and shaped the cloth for the tent, Paul stretched and shaped our love for Jesus who became our greatest comfort and shelter.

So I ask you, "Have you let Jesus stretch and shape your faith in Him so He can become your greatest comfort and shelter?"

BIBLICAL REFERENCES:

Acts 18:1-3

Acts 18:18-26

Romans 16:3

1 Corinthians 16:19

2 Timothy 4:19

FACT:

When Paul mentions the names of Priscilla and Aquila, her name is often mentioned first.

Women were not permitted to teach in public.

Emperor Claudius' expulsion of Jews from Rome in 49-50 AD happened when Christianity was still in its infancy.

Priscilla's husband, Aquila, was her co-worker in the early Church.

QUESTIONS & REFLECTION

Acts 18:1-3, Acts 18:18-26, Romans 16:3, 1 Corinthians 16:19,
2 Timothy 4:19.

1. What gift did the Holy Spirit give to you? How do you share it with others?

2. Which fruit of the Holy Spirit is strongest in you and why?

3. Think of Priscilla's characteristics, which ones do you relate to?

4. How difficult is it to work "side by side" with your husband/wife/partner? Or anyone for that matter.

5. Have you ever moved to a new city, town or country? Was it difficult or easy? Why?

6. Think about Paul and all his teachings and challenges. What do you think it would have been like to be living then to help him?

7. If you could ask Priscilla any question what would it be?

Ephesians 4:11
"And He gave some to be apostles, and some prophets, and some evangelists, and some pastors and teachers".

BIBLICAL ACTION STEP:

What action can you do to apply Priscilla's courage and bravery to your life today?

PRAYER

Holy Father, thank you for always being there for me. Help me to always hear and speak your words correctly. Teach me to always accept your ways and be open to you stretching and shaping my faith. May I never forget that you are my strength, shelter, and comfort; and that I can take you wherever I go. In your Holy name, I prayer. Amen.

NOTES/THOUGHTS

INTERACTIVE BIBLE ACTIVITY

This is an activity for you to search your mind and your heart to respond instinctively to Biblical stories.

For a Bible Study or dramatization at your church, you could conduct an interview with three people playing the individual roles of Dorcas, Lydia, and Priscilla, and a fourth person acting as the interviewer.

To prepare for the interview, refer back and study the previous three stories of these courageous women, including related Bible passages, for insights into each of their lives. This would enable each interviewee to be prepared to answer questions relating to the life of the woman they are portraying.

Below is a recommended script with questions and hints that could be used in this interview exercise.

INTERVIEW SCRIPT & QUESTIONS

Interviewer: "Welcome to the Heavenly View". I'm your host, Pauline Simone Peterson. (note: her name is a combination of the Apostle Paul and the Apostle Simon, who was later called Peter).

Our show this evening will prove to be an exciting one as we will hear testimonies of faith from three very courageous and strong Biblical women. One will share her encounter with Peter and the other two will give us their firsthand account of their walk with the Lord through their relationship with Paul.

These three women all have the distinction of being recognized and written about in the Book of Acts. Luke, who wrote the Book of Acts, recognized their importance in the Christ movement in the First Century AD as recipients of the Holy Spirit. They were active agents, missionaries, witnesses and disciples in spreading the Christian faith.

My guests (gesturing to each guest as they are introduced) this evening are: Dorcas, also known by her Jewish name Tabitha, from Joppa; Lydia, from Thyatira who lived in Philippi; and Prisca, who is known as Priscilla, who is our world traveler from Rome, Corinth, and Ephesus. Each guest will have a name tag displayed to identify who is who.

I'm excited to bring these ladies' wonderful stories about their lives to you tonight. So let's get started right away to see what wonderful and courageous things we can learn from them and utilize in our lives today.

1. Each of you is a business woman, what is your occupation?

2. Share with us some of your strongest qualities.

3. What famous apostle did you meet?

4. When and how did you first come to know Jesus' teachings?

5. What was your "gift or talent" God gave you and how did you use that for the glory of God?

6. How can you relate your God-given gift to Christianity?

Dorcas: "a simple needle and thread could create a tapestry of disciples for Christ, she used her talent of sewing to "stitch together" Christ's love for all people".

Lydia: purple dye symbolized passion & royalty: "Christ's words and life became the color purple in our lives".

Priscilla: tent making/the Gospel: "Cutting the fabric precisely was as important as hearing and teaching the Gospel correctly. Just as Paul stretched and wove the cloth for the tent, Paul stretched and wove our love for Jesus who became our greatest comfort and shelter".

1. How were you instrumental in expanding the Christ movement?

2. Lydia, you are the only one quoted in the Book of Acts among the three of you. Could you tell us what you said?

3. What is unique about each of your stories told in the Bible?

Hints:

Dorcas is the **ONLY woman** in the New Testament to be raised from the dead and also the first Greek Woman mentioned.

Lydia is the only woman who is quoted speaking directly to Paul and helped to start the first Christian Church in Phillipi.

Priscilla and her husband Aquilla are the first married missionaries and they started the first Christian Church in Corinth.

(Note: Think of some of your own questions you might have the interviewer ask any one of the three women?)

Pauline Simone Peterson: "Thank you ladies for sharing your life stories with us. Now I have a few questions for the audience:"

1. What would be the first thing you would say to someone who asked about Jesus?

2. Are there any pastors or ministers today that remind you of the teachings of Paul or Peter?

(Think of some of your own questions to ask the audience)

NOTES/THOUGHTS

Introduction To:
PHOEBE

◆ ◆ ◆

*"I commend to you our sister Phoebe, a **deacon of the church in Cenchreae.**"* Romans 16:1.

These were words spoken by Paul which endorsed Phoebe as a minister of the Church of God. This one sentence is all that is ever mentioned about her. Talk about a lesser known woman of the Bible.

I believe that Phoebe was a very courageous and brave woman, and expanding on her story is an interesting final chapter for this book.

Just imagine if you were her in the First Century AD. You would have had very limited privileges being a woman and, most often, you would never travel without your husband to another country. Phoebe showed amazing courage to travel to Rome and speak Paul's message to the Christians.

There is such a great controversy still in our world today as to whether women should be ministers. I think Paul was grateful for everyone and anyone, even a woman, who wanted to preach the word of God.

Phoebe had quite a responsibility to present Paul's letters to the churches of Rome. We all have that same responsibility today to present God's word to everyone that we can.

Since there is only one sentence about Phoebe in the Book of Romans, I researched many outside sources to see what others knew about her; not much. Thank the Lord that He sent the Holy Spirit to guide me. I relied heavily on Paul's teachings in the book of Romans, as this would be what Phoebe would have been presenting to the Churches in Rome. Here is my interpretation of Phoebe as she speaks to the believers in Rome.

Phoebe

The Story Of:
PHOEBE

Romans 16:1

◆ ◆ ◆

Greetings Brothers and Sisters of Rome. I am Phoebe; I have traveled all the way from Cenchreae. I bring you glad tidings and good news from our brother Paul.

I have the distinct honor of being called the first woman deaconess. Paul singled me out with this wonderful responsibility and acknowledged me with religious authority and ministerial duties. Let me begin by sharing Paul's endorsement of me to you. Paul wrote, "I am sending Phoebe to you, she is a deacon in the church in Cenchreae."

He used this Greek term "diakonos", in order to relate to all of you here in Rome who are predominately of Greek heritage.

Last winter, while in Cenchreae, Paul composed these letters (show scrolls) for you. This was his second mission just before his plans to go to Spain.

In case you aren't familiar with where I live, Cenchreae is a large harbor city in Corinth and located on the eastern seaport.

It is a thriving community of social, cultural and religious diversity. Every Greek, Roman and Egyptian deity has been practiced in Corinth along with the birth of Christianity. Corinth was the perfect place for Paul to write to the Church here in Rome.

Today in Rome, there are five different households making up the churches here. You are a wonderful blend of Jewish and Greek believers.
Paul is writing to you, the "Church of Rome," for three very important reasons.

First, rumors of Jewish prejudice have risen because of Emperor Claudius' earlier religious persecution toward the Jews.

Second, he wants to give you a complete doctrine to follow.

Third, Paul was hoping to get prayers and financial support from all of you in Rome to do missionary work in Spain.

As a prostatis, I am the protectress and the patroness, caring for the affairs of others and aiding them with my resources.

There is so much honor with this title, and I am entrusted with Paul's letters to you, which show that he respects me and finds me worthy to relay his thoughts for his love for Christ and the Church.

There are many of us women who are considered to be a diakonos, a prophetess or an apostle. Some of them you know: Junia, Anna, Mary Magdalene, Dorcas, Lydia, Prisca and Phillips four daughters.

Addressing the first concern of Jewish prejudice and rumors, Paul says, "We are all equal in God's eyes." I will cover that in more detail in his letters. You may have heard that Paul took a vow and cut his hair before returning to Jerusalem.

Some of you may be confused as to why he did this. Many of the Jews there did not like what he was teaching. They believed Paul was abandoning Moses' laws, so he took a vow in Cenchreae and shaved his head.

This was following the Old Testament law pertaining to Nazarites which is found in the Book of Numbers. Of course, Paul only did this for seven days so that he could then partake in the Lord's Supper. For Nazarites could not drink wine or any fermented drink.

Paul did this to gain acceptance by the Jews. For Paul was trying to show them that he could follow Jewish law and still be honest and truthful to Christ.

As the one bringing these letters to you, I will share with you personal messages from Paul as well as explanations and commentary to his letters.

I am not delivering just one letter to some insignificant slave in Rome who will then present it to someone else to read. No! I am privileged to read these letters to you, my brothers and sisters in Christ, and answer any questions you might have.

As you can see, these letters are not just one small scroll. Paul wrote many, many letters of instructions and encouragement to you. There are 16 separate categories in his letters with numerous sub categories on how we should live and worship our Lord Jesus Christ.

Not only did he write encouraging letters, but also letters about not judging others. There were also letters explaining how God is always faithful to us and has a plan for each of us. Paul retold the Jewish history of Abraham and God's promise and the contrast between Adam and Christ. He also proclaimed, "We are now free from the bondage of sin because of Christ. But, we will still struggle with sin."

Paul writes such glorious words to let us all know that we are children of God who is our Father and we should call Him, "Abba". Paul wants the Gentiles to know that because of their faith, they are made right by God through His mercy and that salvation is for everyone.

Paul explains how God wants the Jews to be jealous because they must now share salvation with the Gentiles. The Jews were His chosen people, but when they rejected Jesus, salvation was offered to include everyone else. This was God's plan that the Jews would repent and return to the Lord. Paul further explains that God's mercy is for everyone.

He speaks of God transforming us, giving us gifts to share with others, of loving each other, respecting authority and not judging each other.

And, at all times, we should help others do what is right and build them up in the Lord. He describes problems that the Church faces with both weak and strong characteristics.

Finally, Paul also speaks of his travel plans to Spain and, "longing to visit everyone here in Rome." Even though the people of Spain do not speak Latin or Greek, he feels confident that the Holy Spirit will guide him.

He desperately needs your support, hospitality and prayers for this mission to unfold.

In closing, I would like to read a few more words from Paul. "I commend to you our sister Phoebe, that you receive her in the Lord in a manner worthy of the saints, and that you help her in whatever matter she may have need of you; for she herself has also been a helper of many, and of myself as well".

My dear Brothers and Sisters, I encourage you all to read Paul's letters he so passionately and lovingly wrote to you, my fellow Christians in Rome. This is where you will hear Christ speak to you and guide you.

Shalom.

BIBLICAL REFERENCE:

Romans 16:1

FACT:

The Book of Romans contain all the Epistles (letters) that Phoebe carried and presented to Rome.

There are only 2 lines written about Phoebe.

Diakonos = *deacon (minister)* Paul uses this Greek term to relate to his brothers and sisters in Rome who were predominately of Greek heritage.

In Romans 16:1, the word "deacon" refers to a Christian designated to serve with the overseers/elders of the church in a variety of ways. This is similar to Philemon 1:1 and 1 Timothy 3:8-12.

The word "diakonos" refers to women deacons. A deaconess was usually younger and performed tasks such as: visiting the sick, bathing those recovering from illness and ministering to the needy.

They would also give religious instruction, assist in the baptism of women by anointing them with oil and giving communion to women who were sick and unable go to church. Lastly, they would visit believing women in pagan households where a male deacon would be unacceptable.

Before 49 AD the Jewish/Gentile Churches in Rome were made up of five different households.

Paul's letters address all of the Jewish and Gentile Christians in Rome, not the "Church of Rome".

Anti-Semitism might have arisen because of Emperor Claudius' genocide of the Jews in 49 AD.

Paul had his hair cut off at Cenchreae because of a vow he had taken. Acts 18:18

A Greek prostatis is a female guardian, protectress, patroness, caring for the affairs of others and aiding them with her resources.

A contradiction and controversy arises in 1 Tim 2:10-14, and 1 Cor 14:34-36, where Paul forbade women in church leadership roles. Yet he gave Phoebe the authority and responsibility to act as a diakonos and deliver his letters to Rome.

QUESTIONS & REFLECTION
Romans 16:1

1. What do you think Phoebe's positive attributes are?

2. Can you relate to any of them? If so, what are they?

3. Why do you think even today, women are not permitted to be deacons (pastors) in some denominations?

4. Name some of the other women in the New Testament who ministered the word through preaching, prophesy, evangelizing or pastoring.

   They can be found in:

   Matthew 28:1
   Mark 16:1
   Luke 2:36, 10:38-42
   Acts 9:36-41, 18:26
   Romans 16:7
   1 Corinthians 11:5, 16:15-19
   Titus 2:3-4
   Philomen 4:2-3

5. If you ask could Phoebe any question what would it be?

BIBLICAL ACTION STEP:

What action can you do to apply Phoebe's courage and bravery to your life today?

PRAYER

Almighty God, we embrace how you transform us, by giving us gifts to share with others. Teach us to love, respect authority and not judge each other. Help me to be worthy of your grace, mercy and love. And at all times, help us to remember "to help others do what is right and build them up in the Lord." In Jesus' name. Amen.

NOTES/THOUGHTS

SOURCES

◆ ◆ ◆

BOOKS:

"Holy Bible New Living Translation", Tyndale House Publishers, Inc. Carol Stream, Ill., copyright 1996

Henry, Matthew. "Complete Commentary on 1 Kings 17:1". "Matthew Henry Complete Commentary, public domain

"Phoebe as an Example of Female Authority Exercised in the Early Church", V. K. McCarty, presented at The Sofia Institute

"Nameless Women of the Bible", Rev. Theron Brown, Copyright, 1904, by The Baker & Taylor Co. The Women of the Bible, Dr. Herbert Lockyer R.S.L.

"Really Bad Girls of the Bible", Liz Curtis Higgs, Copyright 2000, Waterbrook Press

"Slightly Bad Girls of the Bible", Liz Curtis Higgs, Copyright 2007, Waterbrook Press

"Strong's Concordance", The Concordance covers the King James Version, copyright 2007 Hendrickson Publishers, Inc.

"Women of the Bible", Ann Spangler, copyright 2007, Mobipocket Reader format.

"Brainy Quotes", Ben Franklin, Internet

Grace Bible College gotquestions.org/Lydia-in-the-Bible.

"Sisters At Sinai", Jill Hammer, The Jewish Publication Society, Philadelphia, copyright 2001.

"What is Midrash?", Ariela Pelaia, Judaism Expert.

"Greek Lexicon entry for Mathetria", Thayer and Smith. "The New Testament Greek Lexicon".

"The New Oxford Annotated Bible", NRSV, Michael D. Coogan, Editor, Oxford University Press, 2001.

INTERNET:

Theodore of Cyrrhus 393-460

Dr. Catherine Kroeger is chaplain and lecturer in the department of religion at Hamilton College in New Hartford, NY Her doctorate is in classical studies and Greek, with a specialization in women in ancient religion, especially women and the ecclesiology of the Apostle Paul.

Aida Besancon Spencer, Professor of New Testament at Gordon-Conwell Theological Seminary, South Hamilton, Mass, and an ordained minister.

Wikipedia biblegateway.com

NOTES/THOUGHTS

MORE TO COME

◆ ◆ ◆

All of the women I have written about in this book showed courage and bravery for the glory of God. They are some of "The Bible's 'Bad' Girls." Their "bad" was **good!**

My hope is that we can all be "bad" like them and do glorious things for our Lord.

I have many more stories that the Holy Spirit has guided me in writing about other women found in the Bible.

Recently, I was invited to be the guest speaker at a three day women's conference in Nairobi, Africa. Just like Priscilla, Paul and Apollo you never know where the Holy Spirit will lead you to share the Lord's word.

God has blessed me with the ministry of performing my stories and songs before congregations, conferences, teas, luncheons, Bible studies, fund raisers and other venues.

If you would like to schedule me to come to your church or organization to perform, please call me at 949-290-0381 or email: daneen.pysz@gmail.com

CD & BOOK INFORMATION

◆ ◆ ◆

Here is a list of my drama stories and songs. Excerpts can be found on my website:

biblesbadgirls.com

Dramas/Stories

OLD TESTAMENT WOMEN

Eve
Sarah & Hagar
Ruth
Miriam
Rachel
Manoah's Wife
Widow of Zarephath
Queen of Sheba
Esther
Queen Amytis

NEW TESTAMENT WOMEN

The Samaritan Woman
Mary Magdalene
The Adulterous Woman
The Mary Show
Elizabeth
Mary, Jesus' Mother
Dorcas
Lydia
Priscilla
Rhoda
Phoebe
The Widow With Two Coins

Songs:

These Bad Girls Did What Was Right
Women of the Bible
Bad Girls
Esther
The 9 GP's (Girl Prophets)
A Gift From Heaven
Shaka, Shaka, Shake The Family Tree

To order my CD, please refer to my website:
biblesbadgirls.com
or
email me: **daneen.pysz@gmail.com**

68021128R00091

Made in the USA
San Bernardino, CA
30 January 2018